THE LIFE OF FAITH

THE LIFE OF FAITH

ROMANO GUARDINI

Translated from the German
VOM LEBEN DES GLAUBENS
by JOHN CHAPIN

CLUNY
Providence, Rhode Island

CLUNY MEDIA EDITION, 2022

This Cluny edition is a republication of the Newman Press
edition of *The Life of Faith*, published in 1961.

For more information regarding this title
or any other Cluny Media publication,
please write to info@clunymedia.com, or to
Cluny Media, P.O. Box 1664, Providence, RI 02901

VISIT US AT WWW.CLUNYMEDIA.COM

ISBN: 978-1685951412

Nihil obstat: Carolus Davis, S.T.L., *Censor Deputatus*

Imprimatur: E. Morrogh Bernard, *Vicarius Generalis*

WESTMONASTERII, DIE 19A DECEMBRIS 1960

Cover design by Clarke & Clarke
Cover image: Rembrandt, *The Storm on
the Sea of Galilee*, 1633, oil on canvas
Courtesy of Wikimedia Commons

CONTENTS

FOREWORD

IN the Gospels we are constantly confronted by the following situation:

A man appears and by his being, by his powerful deeds, by his words in which the Spirit moves, he says: "It is I!" "I am the way, and the truth, and the life!" "Come unto me, all you who labor!" "He who believes in me... shall live!" Men take notice. They approach him, they listen, they marvel, they hope to find help and health for body and soul—and they find both—but they do not understand him, and they turn away. A few of course remain and "follow him wheresoever he goes." They genuinely strive to comprehend what it is that he is saying, but they cannot. His words do make an impression upon them, but their meaning is not really grasped. He lives and is seen, his actions take place before them, but everything remains, ultimately, an impenetrable mystery to the masses.

St. John describes a mysterious scene which symbolizes this situation very well. The disciples are on a lake; a storm is raging; suddenly the Lord appears on the waves. They cry out to Him in fear, but He comforts them, saying: "It is I!" Then Peter calls to Him: "Lord, if it is you, bid me come to you over the waters!"—And Jesus answers: "Come." St. Peter gets out of the boat, his eyes and mind fixed intently on the Lord, and places his foot on the water. It holds! Then he becomes conscious of the storm and losing his grip on himself begins to sink, so that Christ has to come to his rescue: "O you of little faith, why did you doubt?" So long as the Lord lived on the earth, it was always thus. He called, men flocked after Him, but this did not bring them any nearer to Him in reality.

With Pentecost all that changed for the first time, when the Holy Spirit made His appearance in time and human history to lead men to God. Thanks to Him, man really attains to Christ; moreover, he is in Christ and Christ is in him. Now for the first time we have that which is properly called "faith," that is, Christian existence: "the just man lives by faith"; a progress beyond one's former existence: "the victory that overcomes the world"; a fullness of eternal life, but at the same time life attended by all the struggles and tensions of this earthly

existence: "the glory of the children of God" is created, the "new creation" is built in hope, of which St. Paul
speaks in his letters.

It is of this faith that we now wish to speak. Not so
much of the mystery of its divine origin, as of the experience we have of it in ourselves and in others. Faith in
itself is a mystery and must be believed by an act of faith.
There is no such thing as a natural theory of faith by
which it can be deduced from the existence of the world
or of man, for it springs from God's creative grace. Hence
faith, or rather the Christian living by faith, can only be
explained by means of divine revelation. Each believer
can only be understood by faith to the extent that his vision is not lost in mystery. It is not our intention now to
speak of faith as a mystery, but of our relationship to it, of
what we may observe with regard to it, in ourselves and
in others. Not of course of its "natural side"—for nature
and grace are here also inextricably interwoven—but of
that side which can be experienced; nevertheless, in such
a way that in this analysis the essential mystery of faith
stands out.

I

The Origin of Faith

WHAT happens when faith is born?

As a general rule we simply cannot say. There are as many ways for a man to become a believer as there are men. So we intend to sketch in some of the signposts by which we may hope to find our way about in the maze.

We begin with the man who knows nothing about the living God who has spoken through Christ. He lives in immediate contact with reality, with the objects of his inner and outer experience, with his professional obligations, his struggle for the necessities and desires of life, his contacts with other men. His life is completely taken up with these things. His world is a closed book, and he has never felt the need for any other. Perhaps he has occasionally felt that there exists something holy and mysterious, but he has always envisaged this as something belonging to the immediate world itself, pervading and consecrating it.

Or perhaps he may have been troubled by certain questions: life is a mystery and has perplexed him with its "why" and its "wherefore." But it has only occurred to him to seek the answer in the framework of the world itself, in its depth, its height—or whatever word we may employ to describe the direction of a search which starts from that which is near at hand and seeks to reach that which is remote and hard to approach.

He knows of course of the existence of Jesus of Nazareth as an historical figure. He knows that He had great influence and that men are religiously moved by Him even today—but this is unimportant to him.

Things which come from God for the most part come in the form of a beginning. God produces no ready-made events. He touches a living organism, releases a movement, sows a seed. Sometimes the divine action seems to be snuffed out but continues to act in secret. Sometimes it turns up again elsewhere and in another form: giving a new seriousness to a moral conflict; a new urgency to a philosophical problem; or rendering a human relationship more intense, more devoted, more responsible.

This new reality must first be wondered at, viewed as something strange, then pushed aside. But it will return again, stronger, more deeply moving, and inwardly more disturbing.

Perhaps a discussion may be begun of an intellectual nature: Is this so? Is that possible? Is this the true picture? How does that square with the fundamental facts of philosophical or scientific thought? With the convictions of my life? With the views of the times? The discussion proceeds back and forth. But by means of it something else is brought about: the reality of that which is in question becomes more concrete. Its importance becomes clearer, its logic more compelling. Finally, the whole activity of the mind is concentrated on a struggle either for or against the existence of this reality. Actually, thoughts mean much more than they appear to mean: intellectual positions serve, so to speak, as screens behind which deeper, spiritual experiences take place. For some, the discussion may revolve around an ethical issue. An already formed conscience and existing moral habits may find themselves in conflict with a new ethos which has its claims; one may be obliged to defend oneself against something unknown or unusual, which nevertheless has its claims; we may resist the demands of heroism, asceticism, or renunciation, which are inwardly so disturbing... Or perhaps it may be a way of life which is in question: the inner meaning of one's own life until now, certain habits or customs which have been accepted as proper and good, the whole pattern of one's existence...

ROMANO GUARDINI

Or perhaps it may be a question of social contacts, the basic concept of class, family or group traditions... Or, in short, we may have a human existence, received as a fact, formed by education, defined by one's personal activity which has its own peculiar physiognomy, attitude, meaning—and behold something new comes into the picture, something which pretends to be authoritative; at once a conflict begins, either to maintain this type of existence with its customary self-sufficiency, or to sacrifice it.

The debate may assume different forms. It may now be on the offensive, now on the defensive. An assumption seems to be perfectly secure but then dissolves again. A question appears settled but then, after a time, appears to be open again. Something appears to be cleared up; becomes hazy again; and then finally becomes clear once more. Periods of deep involvement alternate with periods of utter indifference. Sometimes a person no longer understands how one who is so cold today, nay, even hostile, to religious problems, could have been so enthusiastic about them but a few days before... But in spite of all these turns, and usually after the lapse of a considerable period of time, the realization finally dawns: God really exists. Christ really exists. The Church has really been founded by His will, and manifests His creative activity in history.

The person feels the impulse to belong. His first attempt may be a failure. He drifts away. He is disillusioned by the signs of human weakness he finds there, by the low cultural level, by the narrow spiritual outlook. He is repelled by what is strange or contradictory. But at length conviction matures and he moves toward the reality which is calling him. This is not merely a provisional engagement, one that can be revised in the light of subsequent experiences, but a final irrevocable decision that he makes. He binds his person, by a bond of loyalty, he attaches his inner being to the reality which confronts him. This engagement expresses itself in a profession of faith, and is consummated by the act of baptism, which introduces the new convert to the mystery of an ever-creative God, in the "rebirth by water and the Holy Spirit."

Now he bears within him the seed of a new life. He stands upon the threshold of a new existence. A new form of existence presses for recognition, and the life of faith begins with all its manifold duties.

But it may also be that the person of whom we are speaking has grown up in the faith. His parents have been believers, and likewise his teachers. His environment has been permeated with the Christian spirit, and the figures of sacred history loomed large in it. His childhood was

passed in the protective atmosphere of a Christianly inspired world. The things with which he came into contact, the events in which he took part, were interpreted
in a Christian sense. He was sustained by the conviction
of loving and venerable persons, and shared their faith
with them.

Then childhood passed. Its protective shell was
dissolved. Things began to appear as they really were,
apart from any Christian meaning, often in opposition
to it. He met men of other faiths or without any religious convictions whatsoever, and found that they could
be healthy, vigorous, effective, often very honorable and
full of character, sometimes much nobler, of broader
outlook, and more courageous than those he had known
in the bosom of the Church. He perceived how often the
great deeds of civilization had been conceived in a spirit
entirely alien to the Christian spirit, or even hostile to
it, and yet no one doubted their effectiveness or worth.
Public life, the collective existence of mankind, unfolded
itself around him; he discovered its richness and vast-
ness, its wonderful creative power; he became aware of
its tasks and allowed himself to become embroiled in
its struggles. It gradually became clearer to him how little it was inspired by Christian sentiments, how alien
the world was to Christ, how completely indifferent the

whole world seemed to be to Him. The Christian element, the Church, according to his daily view of things,
seemed to be something weak, outmoded, bizarre, com-
pared with the immense universe. It was now all over
with faith. He became torn by a desire to be free from
it. Or he gradually drifted away, until it was finally no
longer there at all.

But then, perhaps, after a considerable lapse of time
he came face to face with it again. Under one form or another, everything we have mentioned as occurring in the
first instance could have repeated itself in the second.
Except that the discussions, the advances and retreats,
the alternate experiences of being touched and drawing
away, had quite a different character because he had already really possessed everything, or at least appeared
to do so, for everything is conditioned by memories,
by the magic of childhood experiences, by unpleas-
ant events, by cruel disappointments, perhaps even by
a feeling of guilt. Despite all this, however, conviction
once again was born: God becomes a reality, Christ becomes a real substance, the Church becomes resplen-
dent in all its mystical glory—and finally, the ultimate
step is taken, he binds himself again by the bond of faith.

Faith may either be discovered or rediscovered. In
either case, there remains an unpredictable difference:

what Christian reality is experienced the most immediately or most vividly? It may be Christ whom one first encounters. The seeker then sees in Him the essence of everything, its power, its glory; through Him he finds the Father; through Him he accepts the Church... Or it may be the Church one discovers first, attracted by the solidity of its permanence, the forcefulness of all that it purports to be, the richness of its spiritual content; but it too points to Christ... Or it may be the living God who looms before all else in consciousness, and gradually it becomes clearer that truth and holiness, in their pure state, can only be had from the mouth of Christ, and only in the Church does Christ speak with untrammeled freedom.

There are no prescribed ways to God. God leads men where He will. Always in ways suited to the individual, by taking into account his traits of character and spiritual aspirations, the times and environment in which he lives and by which he is influenced, Providence is already at work.

But it may also happen that there is no break with the faith of our childhood and certainly a genuine Christian education, directed toward the achievement of a proper maturity, ought to aim at this goal. Nevertheless, faith always passes through a period of crisis: faith previously lived in the simplicity of family associations must be wholly reconstituted.

In growing up a young man must assume the responsibility of faith on his own. It is no longer his father, his mother, teacher, friend or environment who are the responsible ones, but he himself. It is he who finds himself face to face with Christ and the Church, it is he who hears the divine word in his conscience, there where no one else can act as his proxy.

He must therefore assimilate what he has heretofore only received, stand on his own feet, take on his own shoulders the burden of responsibility which formerly rested on others; all this can also be accompanied by severe conflicts and by all kinds of uncertainty, doubt, and abandonment; by struggle and attainment; by possession and loss again.

There is still another path to belief, perhaps the most difficult of all. One may have grown up as a believer but in slack surroundings. One's parents may outwardly conform to the practice of religion but largely as a matter of form. One's teachers and instructors may be indifferent; they view the Christian element only as an historical phenomenon, or do not live what they profess. The young man has indeed heard and received the words, but without attaching any meaning to them. He has learned thoughts, but has not perceived their force. Signs and sacred figures have appeared before him, but remain shadowy and unreal.

Around him various contradictory opinions are held, and from childhood he has become used to the existence of different religion beliefs and has not learned the meaning of true conviction or the absolute. It may even be that he has seen the weaker side of each theory so well that he has become skeptical with regard to the existence of any positive religion identifiable as such and demanding a definite adherence.

To destroy this faith, which was often nothing more than a mere faith in appearance, no great shock is needed. It may be sacrificed for the sake of mere convenience or personal reasons; it may simply evaporate gradually, until there is nothing left there at all. And what remains is not any longing or feeling of inner confusion, any sense of religious guilt or consciousness of having important decisions still to be made, but simply indifference and skepticism.

Such a condition is like waste land on which new things can be grown only with difficulty. Thoughts, words, figures, motives, everything has become pale and empty; it is worse than open rejection or complete ignorance. In general, such ground must often first be allowed to lie fallow for some time before it can again be reworked to receive the seed of faith.

In such a case we must exercise patience and trust that God will not abandon His creature. He who has once created may also create again. He has the power to give a new impulse, even when such an action seems impossible.

Whether or not it is a question of one of these typical cases we have just considered, the paths leading to faith are as numerous as men. In any case, that which appears as an advance and struggle forward for man is in reality the calling and leading of God. But God calls each one according to his nature and in his own way.

In the last resort, becoming a believer always means the same thing: another reality looms before the man who was formerly enclosed in his own being, in his own world; before him, in him, or above him, however we may express it—another reality, belonging to another world, from above, from beyond. This reality, this "beyond," becomes more concrete, grows in strength; its truth, its goodness, its holiness become more definite and demand the allegiance of him who has been called. The decision to entrust one's own existence to the strange reality which surpasses it, the sacrifice of one's own self-sufficiency and of the independence of one's own world, will be difficult. It will mean a rude shock and a gamble. Christ has said: "He who possesses his soul will lose it; but he who gives his soul will find it." Hence the soul must first lose itself by recognizing that there is a second goal; and then must recognize that beyond there lies the true goal.

And now begins the struggle between the two goals. They may for a long time remain opposed to each other; each strives to deprive the other of its source of life; each tries to draw to itself the heart, mind, strength, blood. The progress of faith means the conflict between these two poles. There are mutual feints, approaches, and withdrawals; alternate tension and relaxation; until finally both poles coincide to form what we call a Christian existence, expressed by the words of St. Paul: "I live, yet not I, Christ lives in me."

Of course the possibilities for tension remain. For God is always holy—and I am but a sinner. Christ is always the one who comes "from above," from the Father. He can never be identified with what is human. I am of this world, in revolt since the first man. Nevertheless a real unity comes into being. Man is not God, and God is not man. Yet the essence of Christian life consists in man being in God, and God being in man, by reason of the fact that the Christian is in Christ. This is a unity too profound to be explainable in terms of mere natural experience.

II

Faith and Its Content

IN the previous chapter we dealt with the question of how faith arises. We saw how we progress in life toward God, who calls us through Christ; how we adhere to Him; and what exchanges take place between what is above and what is below. We have spoken of how that begins and how it varies according to the nature and circumstances of each individual. We first discussed the man who comes to Christ only late in life; then of him who has grown up in the protective atmosphere of Christian tradition and gradually takes over the responsibility of his faith himself; finally, of the person who in an atmosphere of confusion or religious indifference, with only faded religious ideas or empty symbols to guide him, must renew his faith to attain to a belief worthy of the name.

We have seen how this may come about in various ways, and how, even in the midst of this diversity, the multiplicity of gifts and opportunities may play its part, and have concluded by saying that there are as many ways to become a believer as there are men whom God calls.

But so far we have scarcely mentioned the object of our faith. Now the question arises: Can we speak of faith without speaking of the object of faith?

It has been said that in the last resort it does not matter so much what one believes, as does the seriousness and intensity of one's belief. The important thing is said to be the quality, the force, the depth of the act; the object is merely the occasion for that inner decision and the certainty that comes from it. Others allege that there are many objects of faith which change according to the times and people, according to the dispositions and circumstances of particular individuals, but the essential thing, that is, the religious state of mind, the living awareness of a holy absolute, is the same for all.

But this is not the New Testament view of faith. What it means by "faith" is not some general religious attitude which may be exercised with regard to widely differing contents—much as abstract knowledge may grasp all manner of objects but remain "knowledge." Faith, in the Christian sense, has a unique and exclusive character. Faith is not a mere global concept which embraces a number of different genera: the Christian faith,

Mohammedanism, ancient Greek paganism, Buddhism, etc.; it is a name for a fact which is unique: the answer given by man to the God who came in Christ. This at first may seem like a narrow-minded and intolerant view. Nevertheless when we consider the matter, we can see that even from the natural point of view this alleged broadmindedness or concept of toleration is simply a sign of mental weakness, of a lethargy of spirit. Say to a man, for example, who has given to another not only his respect and his sympathy, but his complete love, involving body and soul and his whole being: "Love is a general feeling which many different kinds of people experience for each other, you, someone else, or anybody at all." He will perhaps look at you skeptically and then turn away. For what kind of an answer can he give to words which wound him so deeply? If he did speak, this is what he would say: "My love is not a mere accident! I do not feel a general love which may be applicable to me or to anybody at all! My love belongs to one person in particular and stands or falls with him. That is its gamble, its pricelessness. That person is my love!" Such a person would immediately understand me should I say that faith cannot be torn from its content.

Faith is its content. It is determined by that which it believes. Belief is the living movement toward Him in whom one believes. It is the living answer to the call of Him who appears in revelation and draws men to Him in grace.

What then is the object of Christian faith? The living God who reveals Himself in Christ. Not God in general, understood in an indefinite sense or as somehow experienced, but Him "who is God and the Father of Jesus Christ."

What sort of a God is this?

He loves the world; He has created it and guards it; He permeates it and all exists in Him—yet He is not the world but exists by Himself, independent of it. Man comes from God; he lives in God and only exists in that he strives toward Him—yet he is not God... God is revealed in everything which exists; all creatures proclaim His glory—yet He is different from everything He has created, and exists in the mystery of unapproachable light, He who is Being itself. God is near, God is everywhere; He is in us and we are in Him; yet the distance of man from Him is immeasurably great, from man's point of view, absolute... God is our origin and the eternal place of our being; our country and our goal—yet He is foreign; so foreign that our heart shrinks with fear before Him.

The image God presents to us is not simple but full of contradictions and mysteries. Likewise our faith in

Him is at the same time an intimate belonging and an effort to overcome our strangeness; nostalgic longing and resistance; nearness and farness; knowing and ignorance. Faith is full of antinomies, full of risks, and cannot be comprehended in a word. It is exactly as God is to us. To the extent that our image of God is simpler and more meaningful to us, so our faith becomes simpler and more meaningful. As our image of God becomes more and more simple—granted that it is a genuine simplicity: fullness contained in a living unity—so our faith also becomes simple. The faith of those who are mature, the God of grown-ups who are on the road to holiness, is completely simple. But it is the simplicity of light which contains in its clearness the whole spectrum of colors; the end, not the beginning.

Yet we must look more closely into this matter. This living God who appears before us in the person of Christ, in His words, His conduct, His being—who is He?

The question, "Who is He?" means: "What does He look like?" When I call someone, he turns his face toward me. In looking at me, in paying attention to me, he reveals himself to me. Then he is revealed to me as his "I"; turned toward me, looking at and speaking to me, I am his "you." Who then is God? What kind of a face does He turn toward me when I call Him? Or, to put it more correctly and respectfully: What kind of a face does He turn toward me which invites me to call Him, while first giving me the sign?

There is an element of mystery in this. When we listen to the words which Jesus speaks, the way in which He turns toward God, the way in which He loves in Him and toward Him; when we notice how in all His being, in His words, in His air, "God" turns up, we then must recognize that there are indeed many faces of God.

First there is the face to which Jesus refers when He speaks of the Father: looming in majesty, the beginning and end of all, creating, governing, foreseeing, guiding toward the goal, who accomplishes what has been decreed from all eternity. From Him everything comes. To Him everything returns. The Lord's Prayer expresses this relationship between man and Him. The parables refer to Him... But there is also a face which appears when Jesus says: "I"; when He stands before the Father, invoking Him or doing His will; when He declares that He and the Father are one, while at the same time obediently submitting Himself to the will of the Father. Or again when He emphasizes that no one knows the Father except through Him, Jesus. This is another face, with different traits and differently oriented. It is called the "Son," or by St. John the "Word." Again there is a third face when Christ speaks of the "Comforter," who will be sent by the Father; of the Spirit who will lead men to the truth of Jesus; who will take from His own and give to men; the Paraclete who will teach men to say "Abba, Father," to pronounce "Lord Jesus," and to "bear witness" to Him. This last is a face which differs perceptibly from the two preceding ones. It is another person; the traits of His face, His look, His breath are different, as well as the movement in which He is found.

But all these faces do not exist side by side: they are contained in each other. The Father is what He is because He is the Father of the Son. He is not "Father" according to the general meaning of the word in comparative religion. He must not be confounded with the father-divinity imagined by various peoples, the Master of the heavens; He is the Father of that Son who is Christ. He is only revealed to us through the Son; only through the Son may we reach Him... The Son is Himself because He is the Son of this Father; His glory comes from the Father and returns to Him; and His whole life is devoted to doing the will of the Father. Finally, in the Spirit, Father and Son are intimately united by a bond of love. In the Spirit the Son has come to us from the Father, and been conceived by the Virgin Mary. In the Spirit He has lived, taught, and acted. From the Father, to whom He has returned, the

Son sends us the Spirit. In the Spirit, who gives the light of faith, both the Father and Son become accessible to us, are present in us, and are given to us.

Father, Son, and Spirit are forever distinct, in the unity of the same divine life; they make but one God, but one Creator, and but one Lord.

Faith therefore means to believe in this God. Christian faith is directed toward God's face, but toward His face as it is. Faith is like Him to whom it is directed. It unites us with God, the One and Three-in-one. Hence it reflects the nature of this God.

What is the name of that process in Holy Scripture which lies at the basis of faith and which creates a new life? New birth. This must not be understood in a poetical sense as a vague expression, but taken literally. The genesis of faith means to be taken up into the creative womb of God. The old being dies, in a certain sense, and a new being is born. This newly conceived life comes from God Himself and means that the believer, if one may use the expression, comes from "the same blood" as God. That is why St. Paul connects faith so closely with baptism, the sacrament of the new birth, which appears as the completion, the incarnation of faith.[1]

1. See the last chapter of this book.

This divine kinship is extended to the three Persons of the Holy Trinity. By faith the Christian enters into family relationship with the Father as His son or daughter; he bows before the majesty of the Father; he confides all that he has to the custody of the Father; he accepts the will of the Father and makes it his own. Such is the spirit of the Lord's Prayer.[2] But all that takes place through the Son. By Himself, the Father is hidden. He is only revealed in the Son whose Father He is. When we are "in Christ," when we look at the Father with Him, when we obey and love with Him, then alone are we "face to face" with the Father and "see" Him. The faith which unites us personally with Christ has its own peculiar nature: it forms a new kinship with God. Christ is our brother, as "the first-born among many brethren." He is our Master, who shows us "the way, the truth, and the life." He is the one who died for us and rose again; who penetrates us by His transformed nature and plants in us the image of the new man, establishing us in the unity of the new creation. Again the relationship of our faith to the Spirit is different. He is the Comforter in us, the one who enlightens our mind and our heart. He brings Christ into us; He teaches us to speak, to pray, to confess our faith

---

2.   Cf. R. Guardini, *The Lord's Prayer* (London, 1958).

and to struggle. He is the flame, the storm, the light, the bond of love.

In each case there is faith, but under a different form. In each case there is a different bond of kinship, but with a different divine Person. Faith in the Father is one thing; faith in the Son another, and faith in the Spirit still different. But none can be separated from the other. The one sustains, discloses, and permeates the other. For these forms of faith constitute but one faith, just as the three divine Persons are but one God.

These are deep matters which become more and more familiar to us as we free ourselves from the impreciseness of general concepts and return to Revelation, resolved to understand it as it is, not as we think it should be in our wisdom or human folly. The stronger our faith becomes, the clearer, the more luminous, the more impressive becomes the faces of God which mark the different aspects, the mutual relationships, and unity of this life of faith.

But with different men it is different.

Some begin by believing in the Father; perhaps without knowing that the Father is possessed only through the Son. For them faith simply means being under the protection of the Father. Starting from that point faith will gradually develop and discover the other faces of

God. Another may encounter Christ first, His historical figure, His words in Scripture, and Christ will lead him to the Father and the Spirit. Finally, a third person is first struck by the works of the Spirit, the aspect of the saints, the voice of the Church. In this way he first perceives the force of the divine, and in the midst of all that is contingent, the guarantee of eternity, which prepares him to bind himself forever by faith. Later the Son and the Father will be revealed to him.

In all this there are no laws. God has given to each one a special nature and mode of life, and He calls each one as He will.

III

Crises of Faith

WE have begun our discussion with the question of how faith begins. But such a discussion can only lead up to a certain point: the ultimate origin of living things remains unfathomable. If one asked a man who is a believer and capable of understanding himself: "Why exactly do you believe?" he would probably reply immediately: "Because this truth convinces me...because this or that value has attracted me...because I see in faith the possibility of ultimate human or religious achievement..." Then he would no doubt add: "But that is not the ultimate reason for my belief; in the last resort, I believe because Christ really *exists*." But that means: "Because I believe." To become a believer is actually a beginning. It is not something which can be deduced from psychological or intellectual antecedents. To be sure, one can always adduce grounds for it, find explanations, or furnish proofs; one can discover psychological motives or appeal to certain experiences—but real faith remains a beginning of an existential nature, and as such cannot be deduced from anything. No analogy can be established with the way a logician draws a final conclusion from certain premises. The process resembles much more the way a sleeper awakes in the morning; or even better, the way a child emerges from his mother's womb to begin his own existence. Faith arises, it opens its eyes, it is born—or whatever expression we may use to indicate the fact that it has a true beginning. Consequently, all attempts to explain it in terms of logical, psychological or moral causation must necessarily fail. In the eyes of the man of logic, the fact of becoming a believer is a circle: it has its origin in itself. But this "circle," that is, the negation of any kind of logical reasoning, is precisely the metaphor which best corresponds to this kind of pure beginning.

Behind the impenetrable obscurity which envelops the beginning of faith there lies an even profounder mystery: faith is the work of God. All those efforts of thought, those instances of perception, those emotions caused by religious values, those encounters with the saints, are the materials in which the true artisan, God, accomplishes his work. Becoming a believer is the effect of a divine action which touches, transforms, illumines, draws us, while remaining shrouded in the mystery of grace. No psychological analysis, no logical reasoning can penetrate there.

But faith also has its purely human side: it is born and develops according to certain laws. It is therefore perfectly legitimate to pose the problem of the experience of faith, and we have already begun by doing so in connection with its genesis.

But in order to avoid reducing faith to a vague religiosity, we have associated the act of faith with its content, and we have noticed their absolute interdependence. Faith is the act which corresponds to the precise reality of God—that is not to say that the general laws and structure of religious behavior have no relevance to it, but the science of comparative religion has made too much of the point and has wished to reduce Christian faith to religious feeling. The important thing for us is its nature; but this can be understood only in connection with its content: hence we have delineated this with care. Now let us continue our discussion and ask ourselves what happens after faith is awakened.

Basically it is a matter of a history, for faith has a history. When it is awakened it is not defined and complete; it is life, and everything living is in the nature of a becoming. Faith also becomes and has various phases of development: it has its ups and downs, its periods of crisis and of calm growth; the becoming of faith is very manifold in nature. Its history involves the whole man, his individuality, his strength and his weakness, his temperament, his experiences and his environment. Like every other history the history of faith becomes lost in the impenetrable obscurity of fate. But, as with other histories, it has certain constant features that we shall note, which will help us to find our way about in the manifoldness of life, without explaining away its originality.

Types of all kinds are found in the history of faith, and one may study it from the most widely different points of view. Let us ask ourselves whether there are any typical crises of faith.

There certainly are, and of the most varied kind. Some, for example, come from a change in environment or from disturbing human events, such as a break in ties dear to one; from good fortune or ill fortune; from physical or spiritual disturbances, etc. We must now focus our attention on crises provoked by definite situations which change the course of a human life.

It has been correctly said that in childhood we are protected as by an enveloping shell. The care of parents and teachers, and in general the spontaneous attitude of every adult tends toward surrounding the child by a protective atmosphere, in order that he may be able to grow up without danger, surrounded wholly by benevolent influences. But the care of adults, by itself, would not be sufficient to create and maintain this atmosphere; there is also needed the active cooperation of the child. It is the child himself who creates this protection, according to the laws of his own development. The way in which he perceives reality—beyond a certain limited point he does not see things at all, or sees them only vaguely—the habit of relating objects and events to his own existence, of attaching a meaning to them or transforming them, all this creates a protective environment about him. Everything tends to be confused. The internal and external, reality and legend, the world and faith all are mixed up together. Everything appears to the child with a familiar and friendly face, everything is ready to help him.

To be sure, it is not always thus. Many children experience dislocations and tensions from an early age. Many never know the harmonious existence of childhood in which they are so carefully screened. They may experience trouble of all kinds: suffering, a sense of oppression, or unconscious desires. Nevertheless, the basic form of childhood existence implies a limited and protective environment, wherein realities are harmoniously mixed up together, in which life in this world and in the next, reality and dreams, soul, body, and things are confused.

This state of mind determines the faith of the child. Regardless of the differences one may observe in this or that child, their faith has an assurance born of confidence. To be sure, problems are always bound to arise, but they remain veiled or in suspense.

Then come the years of adolescence. At first faintly, then with ever greater force and determination, the grand impulse of life awakens in the young man, drives him toward those of the opposite sex, causes him to seek the world in all its fullness; he also seeks his own proper task and the development of his personality.

This drive may be described in various ways. From our point of view the important thing is that it exposes him to the infinite, compels him to rise up and broaden his outlook, to seize the world in its fullness in order to coordinate himself with it. At the same time the adolescent wishes to find himself, find his balance, by opposing whatever limits or restricts him. His will collides with the form of childhood existence. Especially its limited outlook, its friendly protection, the warmth which surrounds it, now become unbearable to him. He feels that its old concepts, its attitudes, its symbols are too narrow

for him; they burst their seams; they must be surmount-
ed or thrown away.

So it is with the life of faith. Religious forms, rules,
motives, everything which has hitherto been considered valid is now felt to be immature, childish, stupid,
and embarrassing: his whole religious attitude enters a
period of crisis which may express itself in widely different ways: in intellectual criticism; in moral rejection;
in a feeling of opposition to the previous generation; in
a revolt against authority; in impatient opposition to the
previous mode of existence, etc. But the essential thing
in each such case is the transformation of the interior life
which seeks room and expression for a new reality in
process of being born. It is of little importance how the
crisis works out in detail: philosophical convictions may
become deepened, or more satisfying moral or religious
values discovered; through new human contacts, models
may be found or friendships struck up which may lead to
a new attitude toward faith. In any case when the crisis
has been finally overcome and has led to a new form of
existence for faith, it seems that everything comes down
to this: the young man recognizes that the immensity of
this vital resurgent impulse finds in the Christian reality
its proper field, in which a free, creative person may be at
ease in faith. He realizes that the substance of faith is not

identical with its childish expression; he rids himself of these and discovers new ones, stronger and more adapted to his present faith.

Then faith develops magnificently; we may consider this its ideal or enthusiastic form. In it the desire for the infinite, the thirst for freedom, and the will to create are merged with the Christian will. Such faith is bold, broad, and sure of itself; it reveals a boldness of spirit, a bravura which enables it to accomplish great feats and achieve a noble strength and intolerance. A life which has never known a period like this must lack something very important.

This attitude grows apace; it lasts for a more or less long period according to circumstances and its inner strength, until it too in turn enters a period of crisis.

This type of faith—like all youthful reactions—has a feeling for the wide world; it has the power to give itself completely to the infinite; is fired by thoughts and imagination, and full of generosity. It does not yet see reality as it is, nor human conditions nor existence in all its harshness. It has transformed all these things by the power of its mind and heart, both of which are inclined to idealize; it has "stylized" them—or simply ignored them. In the same way the passionate will thinks that by the exercise of freedom it can discover its true identity, but does not yet grasp it in its true reality; it creates an identity according to its own dreams into which it fits the transfigured reality. An existence of this kind is torn, so to speak, between the drive of the spirit and heart on the one hand, and the ideal world on the other. But the concrete reality in between has not yet emerged. Now as life progresses, the drive loses its force; the bow of life becomes distended, the power to idealize diminishes. At the same time reality becomes more sharply defined: things appear as they are, men, institutions, situations, and the reality of one's own identity itself. Frustrations and disappointments increase. The compromises which one is obliged to make in place of the confident and bold certitude of this kind of idealism become more and more numerous. A new crisis develops; but confidence gradually becomes weaker and weaker. It becomes more and more impossible not to see the negative side of things, it is more and more difficult to confuse the intensity of desire with the achievement of success. One sees more and more clearly how obscure and stationary existence is, and in the light of this how ineffective great ideals and movements are destined to remain. The meaning of "reality" is revealed for what it is, and how, grounded in itself, it is opposed to all affection and does not yield to the latter.

The danger which then threatens is that of disillusionment: the danger of succumbing to the thought that reality is stronger than the ideal; that actual conditions are harder than thought; that selfishness, narrowness, small-mindedness, baseness and vulgarity are more alive than generosity of heart. The person who pursues a noble aim experiences the shame of being thought a visionary. One who is about to become an adult blushes at whatever remains from his years of adolescence; she who is about to become a woman blushes at what remains of her outlook as a young girl. The danger of skepticism threatens, strengthened by the desire to appear truly grown-up, that is blasé.

It is scarcely necessary to show that faith is the first to suffer in such a crisis. The faith of the idealist dissolves. It appears as overly ambitious, foreign to the world, sentimental and exaggerated.

Then a change may come about in many different ways. The young man becomes more sober in his thoughts and feelings; he becomes more critical regarding his relationships with other persons; more persevering at his profession, more settled in his social habits, etc. Faith may also be re-won in the most varied ways. If it is achieved through a proper deepening of the personality, once one arrives at a certain maturity, reality is accepted for what it is, without capitulating before it, strong in one's faith. Such faith makes sure of its independence with regard to the world. It becomes more deeply rooted in its own ground and may oppose to existence an attitude which does not expect agreement, but extricates itself from all opposition or disappointment deriving from reality, and emphasizes itself, as against such reality, by an "And nevertheless"! Such a person may even find a deep, grim satisfaction in acknowledging that the world does not agree with him, that struggle is everywhere inevitable, and that the life of faith is itself a combat.

We may express this again in the following way: faith grows in character. To have character means that conviction maintains itself in the face of reality. Trust, discipline, perseverance all enter into faith; a tenacious struggle with reality, the maintenance of a position even when a successful outcome can hardly be predicted in the near or distant future.

Such is the faith of one who has matured, of the man or woman who lives by steadfastness without any illusions.

Perhaps the development goes even further. The essence of the attitude of the believer of whom we are speaking lies in the obduracy with which he approaches the real, and in the firmness of his determination to keep up the struggle. If faith is still developing, there comes a time when the believer considers his faith as the most securely anchored reality of all, sure to triumph. He can then defend himself against the reality of the "world" and triumph over it, as St. John says: "This is the victory which overcomes the world, our faith."

To the extent to which a man perseveres and advances in faith, this objective reality assumes a character of relativity. It loses in weight, density and energy. The vital impulse of the believer is not the primary cause here; nor his thirst for the infinite, nor the transforming power of love. But the man who is growing old becomes more conscious of the eternal. He moves less, and thus the voices which come from beyond are better heard by him. Invading eternity causes the reality of time to pale. The believer may relax the tension by which he continually assured himself of the reality of his faith. He no longer has need to rear up against the tenacity and harshness of existence; things arrange themselves more easily; not under the influence of a spell, but through the fissures and contradictions which divide the world, there begins to appear a higher meaning. Existence becomes more transparent, and a new harmony is being evolved.

Thus faith takes on a new form, that of the old man; it becomes venerable and is already transfused by an eternal light.

IV

Faith and Action

LET us sum up the course of our thought so far.

First it was clear that by becoming a believer man begins a new life. Faith as such cannot be deduced from antecedents, rational motives, voluntary acts, or psychological influences. On the contrary, a new life is born with it. A life which comes from God, as the believer himself is aware. Then we spoke of the content of faith and saw how this new existence creates a personal relationship between the believer and God, how it is defined by the face of God Himself: to be a believer means to be in communion with the Father, the Son and the Holy Spirit. Finally, we studied the living act of faith, and saw that it has a history. But there are as many histories of faith as there are believers, for it involves the whole personality of the individual. Faith, like all histories, has its different periods in which the pattern of life changes. In between there are periods of crisis, and many of the so-called "doubts," which we are content to combat, have in fact a very positive side to them. We mean the usual obscurities, tensions, dislocations of life; the contradiction between what is inwardly lived and its outward expression, the inability to understand oneself and to find one's balance under changing conditions. The discussion of such "doubts," one's own as well as those of others, may often be easier and more fruitful if we understand their true meaning.

We must now attempt to understand how faith is realized more fully. And the following saying of Christ may serve as our guide: "Do what I tell you and you will see that you are in truth." That obviously means that in order to grasp the truth of faith, we must not only look at it from outside but enter into it: then it will become apparent to us.

Faith is something which can only be understood by faith. But our understanding needs to be helped. In order to get at the bottom of the "novelty" of faith, we must use images drawn from our experience. We may compare faith to natural knowledge. For instance, the sentence in the catechism, "it is by faith that we firmly believe what God has revealed," seems to suggest a parallel with the act of a pupil who believes what has been taught him by a venerable teacher, who is worthy of all respect.

The comparison is obviously valid so far as it goes. Revelation teaches us regarding the existence of God and His kingdom; we believe the message and are sure of its truth. But the comparison may also involve a danger in that we may understand by this message and certainty something like the knowledge of the natural sciences. According to the latter there are different kinds of matter, different plants, different animals; each exists by itself; it is unimportant whether I am there or not or what my reactions may be; but knowledge consists in perceiving coordinating and penetrating this "external" reality. Who I am, or what kind of a life I lead has nothing to do with it—such considerations are difficult to analyze, have nothing to do with the question, and will therefore not be further considered here. This is more or less the case with knowledge of all the natural sciences. But it would be fatal to apply this image to faith and to think that it could be something independent, without regard to what I am, something that I observed whose characteristics could be listed or classified according to a system. That would not be faith at all, not even if God gave me such information Himself. The image of objective, disinterested knowledge can thus lead us astray.

If a comparison is desired, let us choose another kind of "knowledge," which has more in common with faith:

the knowledge I have of myself. In this case the object of knowledge is not something ready-made before which I find myself as an observer, for here "object" and "subject" are the same: what I know by separating it from my consciousness is myself in process of living. If I do not live it by experience, I cannot know it, since it then does not exist. From this point of view also the external world, things, persons, and events, acquire a special character. First of all they all have an objective existence which can be scientifically investigated, if we may use the expression, but they only acquire their meaning in existence as I acquire mine in relation to them. This world of things and events bears my existence and concurs in its development; in turn my existence gives it meaning and a center of gravity. If I were not living in it or contributing any meaning to it, the world would not be there as an existent.

Therefore if I wish to understand what is truth in all this—I am referring to real, living truth—I must "do" it. I must exist in order to be able to know myself, or know this world, insofar as it is "my" world. I must enter into myself, take charge of myself, live, go forward. The more determined I am to do that, the more intensely I live, the more clearly that is defined which I am seeking to know—namely, myself—in the world which surrounds me. Then only everything becomes authentic. The object of this knowledge is only formed to the extent that I live.[1]

This gives us a more accurate image for understanding faith.

I believe in the living God, one and triune, in His sacred work of creation, redemption, and the consummation of all things. But that this work in which I believe may be complete, I must participate in it myself through my Christian existence. The Christian himself forms part of the Creed. The articles of the Creed are not just so many precise directions written up on the wall; they are the acts of the "profession of faith" of the person who believes them and lives them. Moreover, that person is explicitly mentioned in the Symbol of Faith, which begins with the words "I believe."

The Christian is present in the Creed as one called to faith and answering by faith. And he answers as one who knows that he is expected to live by this Christian truth, which he affirms by confessing his faith. And not

---

1. We are obviously not proposing a subjectivist theory of knowledge. Of course, the world of things exists in itself, independent of me and of my life. What we have said here has nothing to do with Kant. But the world in which I find myself, which is seen and lived by *me*, which gives a meaning to my existence and to which my existence gives a meaning—my existential world, in other words—does not exist without me; and it exists all the more in that I am and live more intensely.

45

as a mere "Christian" in the abstract, but as a concrete person. He himself forms an integral part with what he believes and in whom he believes. The "object" of concrete Christian faith, in the last resort, is only what it is by reference to the Christian who believes in it.

The Greek Fathers tell us that the God of Christian thought is not God as He conceives Himself and appears to Himself, *theos pros heauton*, but God as He is with respect to us, *theos pros hemas*. The God in whom we believe, or more accurately according to the Creed, the God in whom I believe, is the one who has created me. God does not have need of me. He could exist without my existing, of course. But the God who is, is inseparable from the God who has created me. That is why, with all due regard for the supreme sovereignty of God, I must assert—and this has nothing to do with pantheism—that I participate to a certain extent in the meaning of the word "God," since God is the creator. I form, so to speak, part of the halo of God, or of His context—or whatever expression we may use to describe something which transcends all thought. It is the same with the dogma of the Blessed Trinity. The latter is a completely transcendent mystery. It conveys to us the unspeakable profundity of that divine life which draws its own life from itself and has no need of any other—for indeed what could "other" mean to God? And yet, when I speak of the Blessed Trinity as a believer, I do not speak of it as I would of some constellation in the sky, but I understand by it the first principle and ultimate end of my Christian existence, and faith in this supreme mystery also includes me. And the redemption in which I believe is not redemption in general, but my redemption—that by which I have been redeemed. And the sanctification in which I believe is not sanctification in general, but that in which I have a stake.

So it is with everything. God has no need of me. He could live and reign in the complete fullness of His all-holy and unspeakable existence without the world existing, or I in it. This is one of the dogmas that are erected like walls to preserve our idea of God from contamination, from the confusion of pantheism, from confusion with the world. But since God has decreed from all eternity the creation of the world and my creation; since He has called me to return to Him by faith and love; since He has willed a world in which I am to be a believer and which can only be completed by my existence as a believer—the world will only become that which God has willed it to be when I really believe, and by believing return to God. My faith, therefore, insofar as it concerns me, the ultimate completion of the world as God the creator has willed it. And thus my poor human existence, by the sacred liberty of the divine will, is indissolubly linked with Him. I recognize Him, by an act of faith, as the one who creates, redeems and sanctifies me.

To believe, therefore, does not mean that there is something fixed and finished confronting me, which I perceive, but that I experience personally a living reality.[2] The believer who is born to a new existence, thanks to the grace of God, becomes aware of himself in the heart of this existence; he becomes aware of God as the one who dispenses, preserves, and leads this existence to its perfection. He becomes aware of the world as that which listens to this existence, in order to find there, according to St. Paul's Epistle to the Romans (chapter 8), its own

---

2. It may be objected that this is to understand faith in a subjective sense. The second chapter, with which the present is closely connected, should furnish an adequate refutation of this charge. But in order to avoid all ambiguity, I expressly declare that I am insisting here only on one special aspect of faith. A certain one-sidedness is therefore inevitable. For that matter, to believe means first and foremost to believe in the living God, who depends only on Himself; who exists without any need of me; who has created me without any contribution on my part; who grants me a grace which I could not obtain or merit by myself. Thus, to believe means: to go out of myself toward the holy Thou of God. In the abandon of such an attitude, in the movement of release of the heart consists the "loss of soul" by which one "finds himself again," in which salvation is achieved. Everything said above presupposes this and only has meaning in connection with it.

redemption and its own completion. But this existence is only fully realized at its completion: it gains in intensity to the extent that this completion draws near.

We can only believe in such an existence because it exists, and it exists by realizing itself. And the more intensely it realizes itself, the more powerful its presence is felt to be and the more it imposes itself on faith. Again, by another road, we arrive at the initial character of faith, as it expresses itself in that "circle" by which thought returns to itself.

When I say, "I believe in God who is both holy and all-powerful and utterly good"—this remains a mere word, unless I do something about it. In order to make myself fully conscious of the truth contained in this statement, I must "realize" it, that is to say, I must put myself in touch with God. I must seek Him; I must open myself to Him that He may find me, and then in the encounter in which, starting from inside myself, I arrive finally at Him, in which He permits me to perceive His power and His gentleness—then only do those words which connote "force and gentleness" have their true meaning. For they do not mean power or gentleness in general, but with respect to me, toward me, and also toward others.

Take another example: Providence. This is defined as the loving wisdom by which God directs everything. Not the wisdom of the chess player by which he moves pieces on a board; what God directs are free men, endowed with souls. Moreover, namely *me*—the whole scheme of things acquires its meaning from the fact that it goes on completing itself through what I am and do. There is no such thing as Providence in general, but—after God has willed to call me into existence and created me—only the Providence in which I find myself and evolve, which I cannot imagine independently of myself, for in that case I would be placing myself beyond its reach. I can only form a proper idea of Providence by conceiving of it as a continual becoming, that is to say by cooperating with Providence myself.[3]

Still another example: God's love for me. We must for a moment leave aside the meaning of words expressive of the inexpressible, in order to become acquainted with them again from a fresh point of view—how can I believe in this love if it leaves me indifferent? I cannot really believe with all the power of my soul that God loves me, except by loving Him in return—or by revolting against His love. I must love God to be able to believe, with a living faith, that I am loved by Him: there must at least be a beginning of love, or the desire to receive this

---

3. Cf. also Guardini, *The Lord's Prayer*, pp. 12ff.

grace of being able to love Him. And I really believe that I am loved by God to the extent that I love Him myself.

I can only believe if I exist as a Christian, and I exist as a Christian to the extent that my life is Christian—but this life consists to a large extent of faith, for faith is the living consciousness of this existence. Hence I live the more intensely the deeper my faith is—and the circle again is closed.

Thus to believe is not some mechanical kind of an act, but a living act; it is not complete, but in a continual state of becoming; there is nothing guaranteed about it, but it must continually be completed; it requires a great effort, but it is precisely in this that its real greatness lies.

V

Faith and Love

IT is not our intention to simplify the discussion of faith, or to rule out the tensions and difficulties which are natural to it in order to arrive at a cut-and-dried answer. The mystery which lies at the bottom of every living thing is, in this case, particularly impenetrable: it concerns, in fact, a life which derives its source from elsewhere, though intimately bound up with earthly existence. We must therefore expect to encounter a confusing tangle of various psychological forces and motives. However, the fact that the threads intertwine, that the levels are superimposed, that causes and effects interpenetrate, denotes the circle of real life and appears to us as a sign of Truth. When dealing with the fundamental problems of existence, it is more important to penetrate the problem, to get to the bottom of it, than to propose a merely superficial "solution." The latter only is generally achieved, more often than not at the expense of over-simplification, and anyone who has his wits about him immediately senses this and becomes distrustful. On the contrary, if the problem is posed in all its breadth, we are then conscious of being at grips with reality, and we experience a certain feeling of satisfaction, even though we are unable to arrive at any definite solution, in the strict sense of the term. Finally, there are problems—the most profound of all—with which, in keeping with our status here of mere "pilgrims on the earth," we can only hope to live, but not to "solve." Such, for example, is Newman's point of view, when he says that faith means "being capable of bearing doubt."

This consideration leads us to one of those contexts in which principle and effect interlock: the relationship of faith and love.

This is not an idle question. In his First Epistle to the Corinthians (chapter 13), St. Paul links faith, hope, and charity as the fundamental acts of the Christian life; but the Apostle makes clear that the greatest of these three is charity. Actually, how can faith and charity be linked together, how are they related to each other? Does the Apostle not say several verses before this that charity is that which "believes all and hopes all"?

What then is the relationship between charity and faith? The first answer which comes to mind is this:

Charity represents the purest effect of faith. To believe means to be aware of the living reality of God; but since God is love, the believer necessarily begins to seek love. The commandment to love God and to love neighbor as oneself leads us to become aware of and to live by the most profound force which springs from our relationship with God: namely, charity. St. Paul is always speaking about it: in his First Epistle to the Corinthians (13:2), he says: "If I should have all faith, so that I could remove mountains, and have not charity, I am nothing." St. John sums up everything in charity, so that the pressing invitation to love becomes the primary law of Christian life. And St. James does not hesitate to say that the faith which does not manifest itself in good works remains "dead." There is indeed a kind of faith without charity; but what the Apostle says of this shows what a frightful condition it is: "Thou believest that there is one God. Thou dost well. The devils also believe, and tremble." Faith without charity is a faith mixed with terror. Hence charity is the purest effect of faith; it emerges from it like the flower from the stock and roots. But this is still not what we are getting at. One idea dominates the New Testament more than any other, namely, that faith only exists through charity.

Is this not obviously so? If charity is the immediate effect of faith, its efficaciousness or its breathing—then without charity faith would be stifled. Nevertheless, the connection lies deeper. At the beginning of faith love must be present. The faith of which Scripture speaks must have its roots in love.

Is there not a point of contact here with our daily experience?

Sometimes one person may say to another, with the intention of emphasizing the seriousness of what he is saying: "I believe in you." We mean that despite all the vicissitudes, inadequacies, and misrepresentations, we are conscious of his value as a person. We base on this the confident assertion that our friend will succeed in all his efforts. But such a confident view presupposes an attitude of love, for only the look of love penetrates to the heart of being.

Still, seeing is no mere mechanical act. We do not look at the facts of human existence as we look at a board lying in the road. And even in the case of the board, do we always observe clearly what is lying there? Does it not often happen that we miss something, and then ask ourselves afterward how that was possible? Is it not sometimes the main feature which escapes us, while we are deeply impressed by what is of merely secondary importance? Does the subtle phenomenon of vision not depend upon a whole interplay of causes which make it perceive here that which it does not perceive there? Which increases the aperture of the diaphragm here, and closes it there, which sheds light on this or lets shadows fall on that? Does vision not belong to life? Is seeing not a part of the struggle which each is obliged to wage with the surrounding world, either on the defensive, or in order to conquer it? "What I do not know leaves me neither hot nor cold," the proverb says. When one has seen through something, it burns. To know that something exists forces me to take account of it, arouses in me fear or desire, obliges me to act, in short, always provokes a counter-reaction in the one who sees and knows. Hence it is sometimes to our interest not to see certain things, to leave some in the dark, and on the contrary to allow others to become very clearly defined and prominent. Whenever confronted by a man, it is impossible for us to look at him "with indifference," for man is always either our friend or our foe, he favors or opposes our designs, he is a companion, servant, or master, hence all our instincts are at once aroused. Our heart and our whole personality become involved. We can never look at any man without preconceived notions. We behold ourselves, with the burden of our existence, interposed before what we are looking at, like some great preconceived idea.

The time has now come to recall the fact that love, far from making us blind, alone is able to open our eyes; love alone enables us to see someone else as he really is. There are many kinds of love: the love of covetousness and the desire to merge ourselves with someone else; veneration; the love of benevolence with its demands and help rendered; collaboration, etc. But to be authentic, genuine love must always respect the other person in his integrity, recognize in him the right to be himself, and desire that he become himself more and more. By means of this perspicacity love succeeds in seeing the other person as he truly is.

We are unable to say to anyone, "I believe in you," without at the same time experiencing for him a certain love. We now understand better what the word means: we can only believe in God in a living way if we love Him, if we possess at least a particle of love, or a disposition to love.

To believe in God means to have a certain "vision" of Him; to experience to a certain extent that He is there, that the world exists and is centered on Him, as St. Paul says in his Epistle to the Romans: "From the creation of the world, His invisible attributes are seen, by His works, His eternal power also and His divinity" (cf. Rom. 1:20). God emerges from all that is around me, from what I am, and from what constitutes the framework of my existence. But how ambiguous all these terms are! Obviously nature does not reveal God to us the way the needle of a barometer indicates the air pressure. It rather suggests Him both as an explanation and as a mystery. The world speaks of God, but in an ambiguous way, because it speaks through the confusion and chaos of sin. By listening to its words, one man will hear the echo of divine wisdom; another will only perceive cold indifference, or even ill will and betrayal. For the world reveals God, but hides Him at the same time: God is indeed its creator and its model image, but He is also the Other One, the Unknown, hidden by evil. Moreover, when the "works" in question are men, the world of men, or the history of men; when it is myself who is involved—what appears to or happens in me—how dubiously all this speaks of God!

Does God exist? This question is infinitely more vital to me than whether this or that man exists; the view which I have of God depends upon the dictates of my heart, my instinct for self-preservation, the interplay of my desires, my resistance and my fear, infinitely more than if it were a question of the existence of men. The confusion of my human existence disturbs my search for God in the world. And if the world itself speaks so ambiguously of Him—what must the power of a will be, permeated by evil to an indeterminate extent, to hide, deform, and betray the image of God in itself! Hence it has been said with reason: "The clean in heart...shall see God." This is true not merely of the next world, but of here and now.

If I am not at least prepared to love God, I cannot "see" Him. His image will become more and more vague, disappear behind other things, and dissolve into nothingness. It is far otherwise when there is a question of love. "To love," from the human point of view, is first of all to admit the existence of a being greater than myself, who demands a sacrifice on my part. To love means to be prepared to meet the Most High, not to shun this encounter, but to seek it in order to realize that it is only in the gift that this encounter will involve that I can truly find myself. This attitude awakens in me all that speaks of God, and enables me to see Him.

But, God has revealed Himself in a special and precise way in Jesus Christ; so that "he who sees me, sees the Father." In Christ "came a light into the world," this world namely created by the "Word" who is the same as Christ. The Apostle could therefore say that "we saw his glory, the glory of the only-begotten of the Father, full of grace and of truth." For God has spoken; His messengers have brought His Word to us to instruct our minds, to direct and fortify our hearts.

So it is, without any shadow of doubt. With regard to the Son it is said: "no one can come to him unless the Father who sent me draw him." Of the light, it is written that "the darkness grasped it not." Of Christ we know that men have not received Him, they have hardened their hearts against Him. Finally, it is said that the Word of God cannot be understood unless the heart is touched and the mind opened, yet the devil can certainly tear Him from the heart in spite of the most sustained effort.

In order to be perceived by man, the revelation of God in Christ, the Word of God, demands a lively readiness, grace, and love.

Much could be said regarding Providence, the person of Christ, or the Church. But basically it would always boil down to the same thing: only the presence of love enables me to see an object truly. There must at least be a beginning of love, I must at least be prepared to love in order that I may believe.

But how can I love if I do not "see" Him to whom my love is directed? How can I love before believing? We come now to the crucial question.[1]

---

1. St. Augustine discusses this in his *Confessions* when describing his own profound experiences. For a similar discussion of more recent data, see F. Klein, *Une expérience religieuse, Madeleine Sémer, convertie et mystique* (Paris, 1923).

We may say immediately that the disposition to love is already in fact love, and that this disposition can exist even before its object becomes visible. It is the status of a seeking love: the search is still indeterminate, but desires to fix upon some face. The quest, the grasping, opens the heart and sets it in motion. In loving, the mind, polarized by the principle of all love, can already direct itself—even before discovering the truth—toward Him who is its source and its object. The heart can be near God, while the mind is still far from Him. This movement of love prepares man for the total gift which is faith. He opens his heart and will to Truth, breaks the bond of his own self-sufficiency, and brings it about that "he who would save his soul, will lose it."

How does the mother love her child? How does this love come about? He who does not yet exist but will some day be formed in her blood is first of all loved by the mother through her disposition to conceive him. Then she feels in herself something alive, and her love grows in proportion as this body develops distinct from her own. Through this love she becomes aware of it, and believes in the purpose and realization of the existence of this child. And when she has brought him forth into the world and looks at him in her arms, her eyes are then capable of the most profound kind of knowledge, for her heart has now passed through the hard school of patience and love.

God is independent and free, He is essentially "Himself," but He assumes shape and appearance with regard to me; He presents Himself to me according as I am; He demands to be received into my thought and into my life, to become "my God." To believe fully, does this not mean that God has become my God? That He "is born in me," as the masters of the spiritual life say? But this mystery only takes place in love—and the first act of love consists in giving oneself to God in the light of this mystery.

The attitude of love opens the eyes with regard to faith—and, concurrently, the stronger this look becomes, the more love grows and gains in clearness. We could also say equally that faith proceeds from love or love proceeds from faith, for basically the two are the same thing: the manifestation of God living and full of grace, in living man.

Hence we can do nothing better to promote the growth of our faith than to open our heart to love. To be generous enough to desire the existence of a Being who surpasses us, to wish to encounter the Most High in order to give ourselves to Him. To adopt the bold, joyous attitude of one who does not fear for himself, for he knows that the gift of oneself is stronger and more creative than self-containment can be.

But all this remains still very much an earthly matter. We must open our heart to the mystery of love which comes from God, which is given by Him in whom this love is a "theological virtue," is divine energy by which and in which God reveals Himself to Himself: the Father to the Son, the Son to the Father, and both in the Holy Spirit. It is this mystery in which grace allows us to share. God is "given" to us in grace and in love. It is by this mystery that faith lives. We must cling to this mystery if we wish to learn to know a living faith.

We may escape from the risk of indefiniteness and indifference if we adopt a serious attitude toward love there where it is felt most concretely: namely, with regard to our neighbor. The First Epistle of St. John poses the great question: How can we hope to stand in a proper relationship to the invisible and mysterious God? The answer: By forcing ourselves to be in a proper relationship with the men whom we see. Hence this capacity to see with the "eyes of faith" is intimately connected with our readiness to love the neighbor whom we chance to meet, according to times and circumstances.

VI

Faith and Hope

SO far in our discussion we have investigated the fundamental relationship of the Christian life, especially the relations between faith and charity. Hence a new light has been thrown on the nature of faith itself. We have seen that faith is completed in charity: that the latter is essential to it, for the Apostles St. James declares that a faith which does not love is "dead." But the clear look by which faith grasps the reality and meaning of God presupposes a movement of love. Charity and faith sustain each other, and this mutual relationship enables us to see what the common root of the Christian life is.

We must now pursue our analysis of these relations still further and ask ourselves how faith is related to hope. What do they mean to each other?

As with all Christian thoughts, we must first rid our view of this primary Christian virtue of the mass of associations which surround it, and restore to it its original profundity and richness.

We can really only apprehend what Christian hope is when we take into account the disruption or imperfection of human nature. Days and nights pass by, without apparent meaning. Nothing lasts, either works, men or associations. Everything changes and decays. We search for the meaning of our existence in vain. We realize what it ought to be, but we do not achieve this. Fate, necessity, even absurd chance often deprive us of our works, our possessions and our loves. Misfortune overwhelms us; misery oppresses us. When we look at ourselves aside from the illusions induced by self-deception, we become frightened and cannot bear ourselves. We would like to flee from all the wretchedness, ugliness, and evil which characterize us; we avert our face from the other image in which we ought to recognize ourselves, and cast ourselves upon any available alternative: some possession, value, reform or improvement in the world; but we nevertheless feel at the same time how much we are deceiving ourselves.

Is this human nature of ours not something quite impossible, rent by contradictions, permeated by suffering, destined to die, incapable of mastering itself? Yet man is always aware that this destiny ought not to be. A thousand times he has tried to free himself, but he has never succeeded. Should he succeed in escaping from one aspect, it is only to become more deeply enmeshed in another: the steel band which holds him is well forged and cannot be sprung. And yet, in spite of discouragement and despair, the consciousness is always there that he can be other than he is. Of course, such a change cannot come about from the world itself, but from beyond, from something called "God." But how did men come to know about this? Faith tells us about that original promise made to men after they had sinned, and which lives on indelibly in human hearts. Moreover, we know from the nature of the world and the way it operates that there is a divine goodness—in spite of all the absurdities, indifference, cruelty, and malevolence which abound. It is difficult to say exactly how this impression is gained and how it becomes apparent, yet it does.

Thus, along with awareness of his condition of abandonment, man's heart also harbors the certainty that redemption will come. This is not yet Christian hope, but the preparation for it.

It is at this point that something tremendous happened: Christ came into the world to reveal to us what God's mind is regarding us. He did not despise the world; He did not hate it; He was not merely playing with it; He did not regard it from on high in Olympian aloofness, but He loved it.

When we love something it means that we share in its life, by giving and receiving. It is according to this standard we must measure the seriousness of the thought that God loves us. He does not feel merely a distant benevolence for us, something close to indifference; but He loves us, in the strongest sense of the term. That was revealed to us by Christ. It emerges from His words, from His whole attitude regarding men, His brothers. God was willing to go to extreme lengths in His love for us, as shown by the death of Christ.

In Christ, something of that other world manifests itself in the world in which we are. God, who became man, rises amongst us and says to each one of us, to me also: "I wish to redeem you from your condition of abandonment. I wish to be your salvation." To hear these words, to believe in the possibility of this promise and to trust in it despite everything inside us and around us which opposes it—this is Christian hope.

But it is not as simple as this. Of course God is all-powerful; and once we have recognized and admitted that God loves us, we must also suppose at the same time that everything is possible for His love. But we must not make light of the divine work of redemption.

What happens there is terribly important. Revelation tells us that man was lost and there was no way for him to be saved. This was so, before God. But "redemption" does not mean that God eliminates the obstacle by a mere wave of His hand; or that He makes possible, by a sort of sleight of hand, what would have been impossible for man. Quite the reverse! He became man, He entered into this maze of impossibilities and unwound it, so to speak, from the inside. But man continues to be an obstacle and is opposed to the redeeming will of God. The manner in which the Redeemer was received proves this clearly enough. Everything happened as St. John describes it: the heavenly light came, which was capable of illuminating everything, but the darkness did not allow it to penetrate. The hardness of hearts, lost in themselves or retreating within themselves, was opposed to the power of His redeeming love and would not let it in. This resistance was so obstinate that redemption was only possible by the death of Christ. Christ's redeeming will remained—humanly speaking—ineffective, so long as He lived. It foundered on the hardness of hearts. Still it is this very foundering which is redemption; the sign of defeat becomes the sign of resurrection. But the love of the Savior, His light, and His life must pass through darkness. Only beyond death, after resurrection, is victory assured, illuminating the darkness of the world.

Do we grasp the profound meaning of the death of Christ? That He "must die in order to enter into His glory"? Do we see how lost man was in the eyes of God? His condition was hopeless. That appears clearly when, after His conversation with the rich young man, the Lord says to His followers: It is impossible for those who remain attached to their earthly possessions to enter the kingdom of heaven; when the disciples then ask him who can be saved, Jesus looks at them and says: "With men this is impossible, but with God all things are possible." Jesus "looked at them"; that is looked at them like a physician who when asked by a dying man whether he could be cured simply looks at him, in the knowledge of the powerlessness of his art. But in this case we have to do with someone who is much more than a physician!

Christian hope relies on the love God has for us, and on the omnipotence ("everything is possible") of a love which knows that "with men this is impossible," in view of the claims of the world and of existence. Christian hope feels that whatever comes from creation is hostile to it; only God's love is favorable, in the assurance of faith, from which it can confidently assert: "And yet!" Christian hope is essentially "against all hope."

That is why, having its grounds not in the world but in faith, seeing at once what the claims of the world are and yet asserting itself in spite of them, hope cannot be refuted by the world. It has an absolute character about it. It "triumphs over the world" like faith.

Take for example a rocky wall of cliff. It is burned by the sun in summer, frozen by the cold in winter, swept by the howling gales which tear away everything which is not rock; but if a grain of seed chances to take root in some crevasse and a small plant springs up, how amazed we are to see this fragile life growing there where all the elements are so hostile! Is it not the same with ourselves? At the moment of our baptism, a seed falls into our soul from outside this world and grows there. But the world does not care for it. The world is like rock, burning sun, freezing winter, ruinous wind toward it. The world as it is—nature, history, the state, society, human relations—is far from favoring the growth of this heavenly life. Quite on the contrary, everything leads one to believe that it will be dried up, frozen to death, and swept away. But hope is the certainty that this fragile life will "triumph over the world," because it comes from Him who has "triumphed over the world."

But why speak of the outside world? "The world" above all means what we ourselves are: our passions, our indolence, and our inner confusion. All that—more pernicious than heat, cold, or storm—endangers the existence of this fragile life. Let us look for example at one of our days and see what happens, what we neglect to do, the events, actions, and omissions of our life. To what extent does all this contribute to preserve, sustain, nourish and further this divine life? But hope means the consciousness that this profoundly threatened life will persist and complete itself, in spite of the dangers from outside, and above all in spite of those which arise from within.

Hope is always against all hope!

When at the end of each day we look back on what we have done we are always conscious of our deficiencies; yet, in spite of this, we remain confident, for a time at least. We say to ourselves: The next time things will go better. Then gradually we become skeptical and ask ourselves where the redemption is of which faith speaks. Am I not a Christian? It is said that grace is in me and that a new man is to be born: what happens to him? Life passes, its opportunities vanish and do not return; habit, resignation, and routine set in, and we ask ourselves anxiously, if not with despair: Where is the renewal of which faith spoke? This is the time really to grasp what hope which is against all hope means. This amounts to saying that the heavenly life is in us, even though we do not feel it; it grows in us despite all our efforts, thanks to God; our task is to remain calm, be patient, and always begin again. Instances of discouragement, hardening, and frustration are not mere simple appearances but the bitter truth: the blind resistance of worldly reality to redemption. And yet this inner life develops apace, for, coming from heaven, it triumphs over the world.

Here, as elsewhere, it is necessary for us to pay our due to reality, to recognize the real seriousness of evil and corruption. Man must also make his way, plunged in darkness which seems to make the path of the redeemed as impossible as the work of the Redeemer. Here too we must believe. The victory will not be vouchsafed to us in this world; redemption cannot be seen from here in all its fulfillment. Fulfillment will come only beyond the grave. But there is an assurance which enables us to bear up until we get there, namely, hope.

In the last few sentences we have used the words faith and hope interchangeably, and with reason. Faith and hope are not identical, but they reveal, in different ways, one and the same life. This is the life we call faith, in order to designate the consciousness we have of the reality of God in Christ and our faithfulness toward Him. But it is also an awareness of victory and achievement, in spite of an apparently preponderant opposition; it is the certainty of salvation, in spite of the objection of the world which deems the thing impossible. From this point of view, we call it hope.

VII

The Various Forms of Faith

WE have attempted to get at faith from different points of view. We have seen how faith arises; what its content is, and how this content determines its nature; the crises through which faith passes in the course of its development; finally, we have seen what relationship there is between faith on the one hand, and action, love, and hope on the other. We have also noted that faith forms a living whole, and whenever we have examined it in detail we have always done so with respect to this whole. Thus each problem has revealed, more and more clearly, what faith really is.

Now we must ask ourselves the question: Do we always believe in the same way? To be sure, faith is always faith, but does it always reveal itself in the same way everywhere? Or are there actually different forms of the believing man, despite an essential identity?

We are not asking the question in order to find out whether there are different religious convictions, that is different forms of religion. The answer is that of course there are, and this raises another problem: What is the relationship between these religions and the Christian faith? But this lies quite beyond the scope of our book. The difference we have in mind is that which exists within the Christian faith itself. We are really asking ourselves whether faith is the unique Revelation of God in Christ, faith lived inside the one Church, the only guardian and interpreter of this Revelation, can appear under different forms.

The problem is obviously important enough in itself to merit an answer. But from the point of view of the Christian believer we must clarify our thoughts, for if there exists a variety of forms of faith, then the life of faith of a given individual runs the risk of being influenced by that of another, instead of developing consistently according to its own pattern; moreover, we have the duty and the right to develop our own pattern of faith and to stick to it.

It is sufficient merely to consider the men of today, or those of yesterday, to realize how many different forms there are of the one and same faith.

Take for example the man whose whole existence is rooted in his heart. Whether he thinks, calculates, or acts, his ultimate motivation comes from the heart. His heart is expansive, whether in giving itself or receiving in return. It weighs the value of things and the price of existence and wishes to possess them. It wishes to love and to be loved. The question of what is basically true, right, or real is interpreted by him as meaning is there any room for the greatest love. This type of man seeks an object worthy of his love which he can love wholly. Moreover, since love is not something ready-made which seeks an object, but only develops in contact with its object and through it, a man like this seeks to find out how his love can attain its maximum state. To have faith means, in his case, to have recognized that the world can never satisfy him, and that the necessary room for the movement of the heart, the ultimate object and complete development of his love, can only exist in Christ.

This form of faith has a peculiar characteristic about it all its own. Many things seem possible for it which others would deem difficult or impossible. When apparently insoluble problems like the following arise: How can eternal God have created time and the finite? How could He have loved this perishable human creature planted on this atom of dust which is the earth? How could He have developed on the latter a Sacred History? How is it possible for God to have become man? How can He remain for all eternity and yet sacrifice Himself for man? Then such faith has a ready answer full of sanctity: "Love does such things." This is, for such a type of faith, the ultimate answer. On the other hand, this type encounters difficulties where others scarcely see any. For example, it asks itself, how is it possible that everything is not one? That all differences are not absorbed in this one love, that all separateness is not lost in the one fulfillment? That there are so many instances of injustice, pain, thwarted or oppressed lives, so much sin, harshness and cruelty?

In the last resort, the criteria of this form of faith are: that is possible which can be achieved by love; that is true which is believable on the part of love; that is good which enables love to exist and grow. These criteria assume particular significance from the fact that the one who loves is God and that love possesses His holy magnanimity and His infinite power. In this way a perspective opens up, a transmutation takes place of all our value judgments concerning the world which are essential to the Christian life.

Another form of faith is that of the man whose personality is ultimately grounded in the search for truth.

For him the question appears in this form: What are things? What is being? Where does it come from? What is its form or pattern? What is its purpose? Truth for him

is not merely an affair of reason, but that which charac-
terizes existence, the light without which the mind wan-
ders aimlessly, the air he breathes, the substance which
nourishes him.

The mind seeks truth because it can only live by
truth. The existence of things which cannot be explained
depresses him. The obscurity of causes and effects both-
ers him and disturbs him. It is only after having grasped
the central significance of being, and the finality of the
movement of existence, that such a person can really live.
The "truth" which he seeks is not merely the exactness of
a general law which can always be attained, but the sub-
stantial fulfillment which corresponds to his search, the
ultimate explanation, the finality of order. And once he
perceives that this sublime light, this ultimate achievement, this peace in which the mind finally rests content,
cannot be attained from the world itself, he perceives also
that it must have its source in Revelation. That is so, not
because the truth of the world is too limited, but because
the heart demands another kind of truth, the holy truth of
the living God. But this cannot arise from any world, were
it a thousand times more vast or profound or pure than
our own. To know that and to accept it is faith. For a person like this to believe means to have penetrated into the
realm of ultimate truth which, through the intermediary

of Christ, comes from God; it means to have made contact with that supreme truth in its holy essence, its causes, and its effects, to be aware that God is the Light.

This faith behaves differently from that which we have just mentioned. Its crises come from other sources: for example, when certain judgments deriving from investigations in the profane order seem to contradict Revelation, or when a point of dogma seems to be opposed to reason. And it enjoys a different kind of peace deriving from the holy light which springs from the mystery of faith, which alone confers on each being or existing earthly thing its true destination.

There are other men who are inspired by an ethical ideal, or, more accurately, by the desire to do good. They wish to overcome evil. They wish to rise above their insufficiency, whatever is crude, ugly, or impure in their natures. They wish to become sincere and noble. They hunger and thirst after justice.

Or, again, they may have the desire to become new men and thus to realize their true aspirations. Basically—but not always consciously and sometimes in very strange ways—they are motivated by the desire to change, to renew themselves, to conquer and to transform.

This urge encounters limits on all sides; it runs up against opposition and obstacles of all kinds, both external and internal; it experiences its own limitations—until it becomes clear that that image of correct living to which it aspires, the possibility of renewal, the creative and transforming power, must come from elsewhere. The real and essential good is revealed to them in Christ who is incarnate Revelation by the holy will of God, and who, by the grace of God, makes possible what is impossible for men. From this encounter with Christ faith is born. To be a believer means therefore to live according to the example of Christ; to be inspired by His counsel and His commands, His example, and the parables He has uttered. To be a believer means to live in contact with the creative and transforming power of God, and in the hope that these divine forces will bear their fruit.

For other men the ultimate search is for order. They see existence torn by incoherencies and contradictions, threatened by subversive and irrational forces; they ardently yearn for peace, order, and unity.

For them to believe means to discover in God the sacred ordering power, the absolutely just, wise Lord, master of all that exists—and to submit their own freedom to Him. Faith is the attitude of mind which accepts this regulating Power, the divine law which is eternally valid; it means to admit this supreme authority which nothing can call in doubt, and the manifestation of an infallible truth in the course of history. By it we arrive at the possibility of a clear choice, with regard to the will of God. With a joy often incomprehensible to other types of believers, with a true fervor, this type of believer embraces the institutional foundations which regulate the Christian life.

We encounter still another type of faith especially in those persons who find it difficult to express themselves. They have a particularly profound grasp of the inconsistency and brevity of life. What we call reality does not seem to be truly real to them; they consider it rather as a shadow. Whence comes this feeling? Does it come from a slackening will to live, from a sort of anemic temperament, from a tiredness of the heart, or from some other cause? In any case, they recognize what readily escapes men gifted with much greater powers of vitality—namely the contingency and unreal character of life. Such persons long for what can give them a full experience of life, something which is no longer precarious, dull, half-defined, but massive and capable of satisfying their thirst. They wish to attain a reality which has nothing to do with a mere appearance, in order thus to feel truly real themselves. Their road is often a long one. First they may perhaps think that they have found what they are seeking in the passions, in the drunkenness of enjoyment, in the desire to work, in the will to fight—until the day when they discover that all this merely hides the emptiness. This emptiness is found everywhere and cannot be filled by any earthly thing. They then become aware that God alone can heal this wound. He, the essentially real Being, can alone rescue us from appearance. He can bring it about that a finite creature, which is only half alive, can become aware of true life; the break is mended once again and the full stream flows on.

To believe in this case means to enter into the realm of authentic reality and true life, sustained by the hope of taking part in it, little by little. "Realization": this was everything to Newman. To believe means to have the conviction that we can find ourselves there where "realization" is promised.

Faith thus is presented to us under various different forms, and still others could be described. It is the same faith everywhere, but the point of departure and primary impulse are different. Also different are the contents, according to the various personal choices made, but that does not prevent the ultimate object of faith from remaining one and the same and containing them all. Actually, the divine reality which is thus revealed is unique, the all, the fullness which satisfies. But everything in it is not immediately accessible to the individual believer according to his own individual temperament. We can thus have an innate intuition of one aspect or another, the expression of "natural Christianity" in one individual or another. At the commencement of a life of faith it is such a partial apprehension of reality that convinces, first of all, and then remains the basis of faith. Any further manifestations of this reality will remain alien to it, difficult to apprehend and to accept; it will be liable to crises and doubts and will call for a special effort. In all this the nature of each individual will play its part, will determine the difficulties, and will also keep in reserve special forces useful on occasion.

These different patterns of faith are never found in their pure state, for we always have to do with concrete men, not with ideal figures. Thus a single person can possess several of them or perhaps all of them, but in varying degrees; one will always be the dominant form and will characterize the attitude of the believer. Let each person therefore have confidence in the individual nature which God has given him, let him find there the basis for his life and the path which is revealed to him leading him to God; let him not suffer any image to be imposed by somebody else or receive any measure from outside.

These forms of faith all have in common: the good which is asserted, the truth which shines forth, the love which is made possible, the order which dominates chaos, the reality which promises fulfillment. Actually, their ultimate fulfillment does not belong to this world. It comes from outside, from God. Hence each aspect of faith always contains within itself the desire for what lies beyond this world, the longing for the holy, and a disposition toward adoration, but the road which this longing must take toward God is difficult to travel and has its various characteristic forms.

As a clue for describing these various forms of faith we have chosen the notion of "structure," the predominance, that is, of certain faculties of the soul and the values which correspond to them. We could also have employed other clues. We could, for example, distinguish between the faith of a woman and that of a man. The latter is interested primarily in the objective world, his work, his tasks, his opponents, his goal—or whatever term we may employ for this latter—while the former is engrossed in the immediacy of life, in being, becoming, conceiving and bringing forth, protecting, nourishing, sympathizing, and assuming, and lives in a more profound world, one subject to rhythms and symbols. These two kinds of human being each develop his own faith in his own way. The structure of faith will be one thing for those who educate, teach, heal, assist, serve, and something different for those who fight, conquer, reign, etc. The fact that we are members of this or that people will have its bearing on the form of our faith—to such an extent that the type of faith and devotion peculiar to a neighboring people may seem disconcerting to us; it may appear strange and even hostile, impious and contrary to the Christian spirit. It is the same with different age-groups and their peculiar characteristics, with different strata of society, intellectual levels, professions, etc. The faith of the priest, for whom the reality of religion itself constitutes the content of his vocation, will manifest itself differently from that of the layman. The latter lives in the world and is centered upon the world; he encounters religion under different auspices, isolating certain features and subjecting them to the practical.

I should like to draw your attention to another difference which seems to me to be particularly important. Namely, that between two kinds of faith: an abundant or full faith, and an empty faith. The first is characteristic of those who have an immediate and lively awareness of the contents of faith. Not that they must necessarily be particularly pious or profound people—in that case it would no longer be a question of the "structure" of faith but of its seriousness—but they do have the gift of being particularly sensitive to what is alive in everything they encounter. Things, ideas, events all speak to them. It is the same with their faith. They feel what they believe. The person of Christ, the details of His teaching, the possibilities of an eternal destination, all these things move them, overwhelm them, frighten them, console them and gladden them. The life of their faith, developing along different lines, may be either simple or richly unfolded, profound or superficial, elevated or vulgar— but it is always the Christian reality which touches them and acts upon them directly.

The attitude of the person with an empty faith is quite different. In his case, the objects also exist, but the soul remains cold. It recognizes that there are values, but does not experience them directly. Goals are defined, decisions reached, the will sets itself in motion, works, struggles, makes an effort, but there is no special feeling of engagement. There is no doubt but that the destination will be reached, but the mind remains indifferent. The person knows, conceives thoughts, chooses, acts, but only with premeditation, discipline, and effort. The basic nature of one's being remains unmoved. The space seems empty. Realities have no density. Truths seem to be but words.

One is at first inclined to say that only the first attitude is that of a believer, the second being merely

indifference, lassitude, coldness, spiritual anemia, etc.
Such a judgment would not only be superficial but false.
Faith is present here, too, but under a different exterior.
In the former case, faith is borne by inner experiences
which give it warmth, proximity, and richness, but also
run the risk of making it illusory, deceptive, shallow or
adulterated. The second attitude is characterized by
emptiness, still in this emptiness a spiritual meaning is
perceived which serves as a basis. The soul is not moved
by any ardor; but this aridity itself is something valorous.
Whatever is done is done voluntarily, with difficulty, and
there is in this a great purity. Such a laborious attitude
may serve as a beginning for something truly genuine
and noble.

The difference is important, for it seems that today the second of these attitudes is the most prevalent.
Perhaps we are passing through a phase from a faith of
richness to one of poverty? Religious art and the new
churches seem to indicate this, for their simplicity cannot be explained by the mere taste for novelty, or by a
lack of means, but is a witness to a profound change
in the attitude toward faith. When the rooms are empty and the walls bare, a faith is expressing itself in fact,
which, in the "emptiness," the bare space, the plain sur-
faces, wishes to express the spiritual manifested in pure

objectivity without losing itself in a wealth of detail; it is a faith which has no need for support and is capable of triumphing despite the poverty of means. After the luxurious use of symbols, images, and forms of past ages, there is emerging a form of faith which longs for simplification, for a return to the sources, for conciseness. Multiplicity has become strange to it; the possibility of finding a satisfactory explanation for everything leaves it perplexed. It hankers after an impoverished and simple life, with its righteousness. So long as we do not make this trend into a special "religion," nor become intolerant with regard to other forms of faith, this attitude is a fine thing and can play a vital part in Christian experience.

All these considerations add up to one important fact: faith exists under different forms according to the temperament and capacity of each individual, the structure which is characteristic of him, his state of life, a given people or age. These forms represent to a certain extent the terrain in which faith lives. They determine the particular form of its development in accordance with the resources and difficulties peculiar to each one and the duties which are set before him. In them there is expressed, we might say, the particular vocation which the faith of each one will assume. But the fundamental kernel of faith, that which the Scripture means when it says: "he who believes...shall be saved, but he who does not believe shall be condemned," is necessarily distinguished from these particular forms. Faith itself consists in the fact that the kernel of man, his "identity," stripped of everything, his "heart of his heart," is called by God, apart from all structures, and that he has responded to this call. The ultimate of faith is not structure; it is obedience and faithfulness.

And this leads us to draw another conclusion regarding faith—namely, that men have different aptitudes which manifest themselves differently in varying degrees. In particular there is a "religious" attitude, that is, an inclination to perceive the invisible in the midst of the visible, the eternal through the finite and the ephemeral. What is attained in such case is not "truth," nor "the good and the just," nor "beauty," nor "order and measure," nor any "profane" value, but the "sacred" (taking this word in its most obvious meaning, as employed by comparative religion). Other values are perceived, but only to the extent that they are bearers of the "sacred" or holy, that is, as holy truth, beauty, or order. This religious sensitiveness consists in a sort of respect or veneration, a gift of sympathy which is called "piety." At first sight this would seem to be a structure like the others. It has its peculiar characteristics: height and depth, width and intensity, plurality and simplicity. In it we may find persons who are specially gifted or creative geniuses; ordinary persons who are more conformist; finally others who are only modestly endowed and lacking in all sensibility. We encounter spontaneity and laborious plodding, purity and impurity, the genuine and the artificial, procedure, routine—in short, the whole gamut of values, both true and false. But then we ask ourselves: What is the relationship between all this and what Christ calls faith? Between all this and what determines the salvation or loss of mankind?

This question is of the greatest importance. Our times are busy investigating the structural formation of life with ever-increasing insight; we have evolved religious psychology, sociology, etc. But if we were to identify faith with a religious inclination, there would be natural believers on the one hand and natural unbelievers on the other! True, this opinion is current at the present time; but if this were so, the message of Christ for men would be matter of individual talent or appeal. No— the faith of which Christ speaks has nothing to do with disposition. The essential lies beyond whatever is within the purview of psychology and rises straight from the inner being of man to God. According to its manifestations, acts, or attitudes, faith flows in structures according to the predispositions of different individuals; but the call of God affects one elsewhere, and the decision to be made lies elsewhere. We may perhaps distinguish between the "body" and "soul" of faith. The body of faith differs according to various dispositions, countries, ages, and human circumstances; but its soul—or more exactly the seat of its soul—is everywhere independent of determinations. At this depth—as we have already noticed—there is only pure encounter between the human identity and God. Through all the variations of structure and aptitude, this supreme encounter is the essential thing.

As for the religious attitude, this does not belong to the "soul" but to the "body" of faith. True, there is a faith characterized by such a disposition, rich, creative, abundant in resources, but it lies exposed to a definite danger: for the very inclination which can lead toward faith can also and equally well lead to doubt. It may render one unstable, eager for religious impressions, exaggerated and fanatical. The absence of a religious disposition, on the other hand, may be an obstacle: it may mean that there is no urge, no depth, no impact, no "experience." Yet, such a faith is loyal, faithful, disinterested and solid. Moreover, the divine origin of faith is revealed by its capacity to assess immediately whatever derives from spontaneous tendencies or from environment, even a

Catholic one. Faith is quick to detect whatever is suspect, reveal its limitations, attachments, and worldly contaminations, or unmask the illusions, sometimes extremely well hidden, to which these dispositions external to itself are prone.

And if it is true that the religious disposition needs to have certain individual or social presuppositions, or that under the influence of a particular culture the religious awareness may decline or even disappear; if there really exists the person who can do without the "holy"—yet we must nevertheless remember that the ultimate decision relative to God lies quite outside this whole order of aptitudes and dispositions. It is perhaps externally unverifiable, and even the individual himself may not be fully aware of what is taking place within him, of its Christian meaning, of that relationship, that is, between the human identity stripped of everything and God.

This last point is of course the very object of faith. The vital point, independent of all structures, is to know that in each being, regardless of his individual dispositions and from beyond them, God is calling and that he has answered, aside from all conditions and circumstances. That this call exists, each one of us can only believe and must do so. "God wishes all men to be saved"—even those who are poorly endowed from the religious standpoint! The man who finds himself in the latter situation, forced to lead a hard life, full of renunciation from the spiritual point of view, if he truly tries to have faith, will remain in God's eyes a believer, in spite of all the dryness and desolation. To believe this is of course a matter of faith, of faith mixed with hope. But such a person can in the end only believe, and must.

VIII

Knowledge in Faith

ST. Anselm of Canterbury, in his profound work enti-
tled *Proslogium*, says: "Without experience, no knowledge; but without faith, no experience." This sentence
establishes a kind of chain: faith is the beginning and
makes experience possible. Finally, experience begets
knowledge. Misunderstood, the sentence could lead us
to separate forces and events which in reality form a living whole. Properly understood, it helps us to discover a
new aspect of faith.

St. Anselm first of all poses a "faith" which does not
yet "know." Owing to a variety of circumstances man encounters the word of God and trusts it. Actually, there is
already here a question of "knowledge"; I must have at
least arrived at the conclusion that in the Church and in
its teaching, in the witness of the messengers of God, in
the person of Jesus Christ, we have to do not merely with

a human wisdom which speaks, however profoundly, but of a divine wisdom. I must realize that there is more involved here than merely a religious emotion: namely, a divine gift, an explicit advent of God in time. Nevertheless, according to Anselm, this knowledge is only preparatory, it leads me to that decision which is important above all else: to trust in God who is speaking, to listen to His call, to submit myself to His will, to bind myself to Him in loyalty. I accept what He tells me; I welcome what He reveals to me about Himself. This obedience to the word of God is the root of faith.

But this faith, according to Anselm, does not yet "know." It does not yet understand its content. There is, of course, a certain knowledge. To a certain extent faith must have understood its content, since to recognize that it is God who is speaking here means to recognize who God is and who man is in relation to Him. And yet—the core of the decision, the root of faith is, on the basis of a simple word which one believes, to accept without reservation the mystery present here and make it the beginning of a new life.

Then the seed thus received begins to sprout. The believer penetrates the content of faith, seeks to understand its profound meaning and internal structure, to take stock of the demands which it involves. Little by little he progresses from simple obedience to an inner knowledge of what has been revealed. He desires to pass, according to the terminology of ancient philosophy, from *pistis* to *gnosis*. And he does so not with the natural understanding, limited by this world, but with a cognitive faculty which proceeds itself from illuminating grace. Moreover, the eye of faith opens to the light of grace and grasps all the more clearly this reality of God which is revealed. Such a knowledge is nothing but the growth of faith.

But this knowledge takes place in "experience," that is in the concrete approaching, probing, getting the feel and the taste of something. It is only in this way that the content of faith flowers, like a bud, full of truth and value; it presents itself clearly to the mind and penetrates to the very heart.

Yet faith does not cease to be faith. It never is transformed into knowledge in the human sense of the word, nor even into that higher knowledge which is the result of a developed consciousness. Fundamentally faith is the obedience of man to God, the holy and incomprehensible one, the attentive submission of finite humanity to the reality of its Creator and Lord who, in revealing Himself, has disclosed man's sinful state and nothingness. There is a gulf of dissimilarity here which nothing can fill; faith always remains the obedience acceptance of the incomprehensible reality of God toward which humanity is directed. This obedience would be abolished if man should arrive at an exhaustive knowledge of the reality of God, for such a knowledge would be a possession or a domination. The only knowledge possible is founded on obedience. It comes from that acceptance we mentioned above, and which abandons the glorification of self. It is achieved in the constant abandonment of self to the judgment of Holy God. Knowledge in faith, according to the nature and object of faith, is extinguished as soon as faith is extinguished. It is nevertheless a genuine knowledge, a living "knowledge," in the sense of an inner presence, a penetration.

We have repeatedly said that these two things cannot be envisaged separately. When the mind and heart are inclined to this obedience, it is by virtue of a light from a certain "knowledge" springing from grace, the first premonition of faith. Faith cannot be blind. Here again there is a certain kind of experience, "a manifestation of power" intimately felt by the one who believes. The one is always borne by the other, for what is awakened and develops forms a whole. Nevertheless, the aphorism of St. Anselm is very significant. It sheds light.

We shall now speak about this experience, the beginning of knowledge. Not about it in general—a whole lifetime would be necessary for that—but about certain aspects of it.

Experience, for the believer, means to live with the realities, the forms, the events, the values which constitute the content of his faith; it means to adopt this whole content, to preserve it in consciousness, to reflect on it, to recur to it throughout the various circumstances of one's life and thought, until finally it discloses itself to the believer. The believer then sees the content of his faith. Actually, the teachings of faith have nothing to do with scientific propositions. As soon as I understand what the relationship is between one mathematical quantity and another, the matter is clear. When I know that one element combined with another forms a given compound, I seek to know no more. When historical sources worthy of credit teach me that someone has lived at a certain epoch, that he did this or that, the matter is closed. But it is not the same with faith. It is a question here of "profound" truths, and of a living "profundity" which only describes itself slowly. No, I ought rather to speak of a holy profundity which only reveals itself in definite circumstances, for it presupposes definite states of knowledge and attitudes: this is precisely the meaning of "experience." Thus, faith assures me that God loves man. I can accept this simply as the child does who is convinced that the Good Lord is well disposed toward him. But the profound meaning and consequences of this assertion are only revealed to me slowly. In order to penetrate it I must first understand what "man" is: that being who is such a mixture of good and bad, so full of contradictions, strange, insignificant, hopeless, and yet so great. I must learn what life has to tell me about human existence, its challenges, its destiny. This lesson of course cannot be learned simply from human wisdom. It lies at the bottom of faith and is only possible for one who looks, judges, and acts as a believer. The latter alone can sound the depths of that phrase: God loves man.

It is the same with the other elements of the content of faith. I must live with them every day, and depend on them. They must be at once the circumstances, the causes, and the goals of my life. Then they will reveal themselves to me, their profundity will become meaningful, their inner relationships will become more definite, the truth will become manifest. It is thanks to such experience as this that knowledge in faith develops: holy knowledge, the fruit of grace.

The truths of faith are not mere facts which can be grasped only in a purely theoretical way. If this were so, they could be probed by means of research and study. On the contrary, faith means that man gets at reality, and that this requires a definite action, aimed at God as source and end. Man will receive power to dominate life. But all this business of requirements, inspirations, spiritual forces only becomes intelligible to the extent that one tries them.

I really do not understand the road map which I have brought along with me unless I verify the meaning and significance of each mark and symbol on the spot, and can thus find out what credit I am to repose in them. The safeguards which a boat offers in case of danger, the possibilities there will be of moving or holding out, can only be determined once I have embarked. Hence in order to recognize the content of faith we must first experience it. "If you abide in my word...you shall know the truth." If for example I am told that everything which happens is owing to Providence, that over the whole life of man and over each detail of this life there is the hand of God, this assertion will remain a dead letter as long as I have not experienced it. Only when I decide to consider everything which happens to me, both the good and the bad, as coming ultimately from God, do I understand what that means. This is easy to say but difficult to do: infinitely difficult for the human will in despair about its own powerlessness and yet obstinately at grips with it, so lazy and lax, yet so rebellious and proud. But it is only when I act thus, and to the extent that I really do so, that this be-lief in Providence is revealed to be true. It is only when I am quite convinced that I have received a special mission from God, that every event offers me the opportunity of fulfilling it. It is only when I persevere in this conscious-ness, through joy and sorrow, through success and fail-ure, that I become aware of the existence of a force which directs and sustains me—and this is precisely the "truth" of faith which we mean here.

Such then is the unfolding of experience: the thoughts of faith are embedded in the matter of existence; we have guided our life according to them; their content has re-vealed itself, and faith has gained in knowledge.

I do not believe in ideas but in realities. God in whom I believe is not the idea of supreme value, the idea of holy justice, or anything of that sort. He is real. This term "real" aptly expresses what it means: the ground I stand on is real; the wall I bump against is real; the men I fight are real; the power of the mind which distracts or inspires me is real. God is real—of course in a different sort of way. He is real in that He is Being in itself, the Holy One in whose sight our existence appears as sinful and futile: the Creator and the Lord. And Christ is real. He is not only the idea of the Man-God. Were He only that, He would be lacking in power. But He is really the

Son of God "yesterday and today and forever," living and present. And the influence which He exercises throughout history is real, in the Church, in each soul. Not only in the thoughts, the feelings, or the experiences we have, but in the "new birth in the Holy Spirit," and "growth" toward the glory of the children of God.

To believe is to be bound to this reality. Is it possible for me to preserve faithfully the content of this faith, to concern myself about it, to conform my life to it, unless the realities which are included in it and which are important are manifested to me? God loves me, does He not? Is it for me that Christ has come—is it possible then that He is not revealed in me? Let us not ask ourselves how this can be or cannot be—though it is impossible for me to search painfully for God according to His will unless He, all-loving and all-powerful, grants me an inner perception of His holy reality; unless in His love, He knows that it is better for me to persist in the difficult effort of "pure faith," or, in His justice, imposes upon me this trial because of my sins!

There is also another experience, the most profound of all: holy realities become realities. This is what Cardinal Newman meant when he spoke of "realization," that is, such realities leave the realm of thought, intention, or will, to become a living presence or acquire real destiny. But this may take a long time, a very long time. It may happen that certain persons plod along for many years in the service of pure faith, troubled and from afar. But then there comes a day when it is no longer the man who bears faith but his faith which bears him. What is contained in the New Testament is written "for our enlightenment." Yet, how different the faith of the men of those times was from the difficult, remote way in which we "believe firmly" what is revealed and taught us! Men of those days suffered, were persecuted, struggled, failed, were even condemned to death sometimes—but a holy reality touched them, shook them, made them enthusiastic, or crushed them. This is written for our benefit, too.

It is all this and much more that this phrase ought to mean: faith must grow from experience to knowledge. We have to do with the inner history of faith, which is unfolded when the believer lives with the object of his faith. In his daily life he encounters the contents of his faith; sometimes one aspect or another is revealed to him more clearly; the deeper levels begin to appear more distinctly; the object of faith is seen both as a suggestion and demand: he becomes aware of what it requires of him. He directs his life according to his faith, he molds his life according to it, he makes it the standard of his existence. Thus he comes to know what the powers contained in his faith are, how it assures him stability, support, and security. What he received first as teaching, story, message, changes in consistency, density, and weight; it is found to be reality. All these things are in keeping with human experience: action, life, challenge and bold decisions; but in all this it is God who is acting, for faith is grace. The light of God develops the content of belief in knowledge. Under the guidance of God the obedience of faith finally arrives at joyful possession. God Himself, the all-holy, is revealed as a living reality in that which obedience has enabled us to retain and to think.

It may even happen that this knowledge in faith assumes the particular form which St. Bernard of Clairvaux has called the *cognitio Dei experimentalis,* or "knowledge of God by immediate experience," and which can loosely be called mystical.

Learned investigations have been concerned with the question whether there can be an immediate experience of God or not; whether such an experience is exceptional or found in the normal path to faith. Some have portrayed the mystical experience as something of dubious value, dangerous for the purity and integrity of the Christian faith. Others have seen in it something interesting from the psychological point of view, or as an object of literature or amusement, or as a religious *curiosum,* etc. All such attitudes leave out of account the Christian evidence which is based on Scripture, the lives of the saints, the conscience of a believing people: namely, that God is the living God, and in Christ God is near at hand. That it is in Him that "we have movement, life, and being." That He is love and liberty and grace—and that no power of this world, no scientific theory, no theological syllogism can prevent Him from touching the soul when it pleases Him. A faith which has been assumed humbly and seriously; a faith which receives from God the longing for the immediacy of love and which has not let this longing die, but which has unceasingly prayed for the fulfillment of this desire, however long the waiting period may be; a faith which is not content with temporary satisfactions, but with the confidence of the child of God remains anchored in the essential; such a faith doubtless always ultimately arrives, more or less, at that which we mean by the "mystical," unless we prefer to speak simply of the fullness of faith.

Thus we come back to what has already been said and which must be said again and again by way of conclusion: faith always remains "faith."

Despite all progress in the realm of knowledge; despite all experience, however strong and rich it may be, which causes man to pass from *pistis* to *gnosis*, such a knowledge always remains a knowledge of faith, faith is never replaced by an immediate knowledge. We always have to receive in ourselves this truth by means of Christ, receive revelation from God. Our task is always the humble and courageous one of listening obediently and acting boldly.

IX

Faith and the Church: Dogma

IF a man living in the first centuries had been asked: "What does the Church mean in your faith?"—he would perhaps have answered: "The Church is the mother who has borne me; it is the air I breathe, the ground on which I walk. Indeed, it is the Church itself which believes: it is its faith which lives in mine." We modern men no doubt do not see the question in this light. While fully understanding and approving such an attitude, we must approach the problem from a different point of view. The West is now emerging from a process of individualization in which the individual has emancipated himself from the bonds of the community in order to find his own basis in himself. We all know that this tendency has been deplorable in many respects. It has made an impression on our thought, opening up certain avenues to truth, but at the same time exposing us to error. Though

we have been obliged to retreat somewhat, we must nevertheless take into account this individualistic tendency
and may even employ it as a starting-point.

When we wish to get at the bottom of faith, we quite
naturally appeal to the situation of the individual who is
confronted by this problem in his conscience: "Is it God
who is speaking here? Ought I to believe, or am I justi-
fied in following my own personal inclinations? Should
I take the step of faith, or should I remain oriented in
myself?" The loneliness in which the conscience must
decide to assume the responsibility of faith, the boldness
which this step requires, the steadfastness and will with
which the decision must be maintained—all this points
to the seriousness of faith. The individual knows that he
stands by himself. No one can make the decision for him.
He must triumph over the conflict between faith and his
soul, his life, the world: no one else can do this for him.

All this is very true and may lead to emphasis upon
the very modern idea of solitude and self-domination.
But we must ask ourselves a question: You who speak
this way—where does your faith come from? Have you
derived it from yourself? Or have you received it directly from God? Of course you have not! Your parents
have raised you. Your teachers have taught you. You have
learned about it in books. You have received your faith

from the practice of faith in your parish, from the traditions of your environment. You have received not merely certain contents, certainly purely objective doctrines, which it is up to you to transform into faith or to refuse to believe as the case may be, but your faith itself as a way of life both for mind and heart has been kindled in you by the faith of others. Doctrinal instruction by itself is incapable of awakening faith in the hearer, only doctrine in which the teacher himself believes. It is when truth is loved and lived that it awakens faith. It is the faith of your mother, or your teacher, or your friend, or some other person around you, which has awakened your own. At first, without knowing it, you have lived with them in their faith; then your own faith arose, became definite, and finally found the strength to stand upright. Just as a candle is lit by contact with the flame of another candle, so faith kindles faith.

Of course it is God who makes faith. He draws the heart; He touches the spirit. He draws the seed of a new life from some word which is heard, from some figure encountered, from some picture looked at. It is God who calls the individual—but He calls him as man, inextricably bound up with the maze of associations necessary for life. Man is for man the road to God; the individual separated from his environment simply does not exist.

These associations are so powerful that it is easy to recognize in our faith the attitude of those by whom it has been awakened: the way in which our teachers have conceived divine truths; the way in which a friend has imagined a holy life; the motives which have played such an important part in the life of the person who touches us so deeply; the emotion displayed by a family in celebrating a feast-day; the profound seriousness, unmindful of her own great sanctity, with which our mother used to pray, and the persistence which she derived from her trust in God—including also the feelings of like or dislike or even revulsion which characterized the atmosphere of our childhood, as well as the special customs of our social environment or local traditions.

It is God who makes faith. It is He who awakens faith in the heart of the one whom He calls. He may inflame a heart in an environment that is completely dead. It may cause the flame to spurt up on contact with a word in the air, or with nothing at all. "God is able out of these stones to raise up children to Abraham"—and this is basically what He always does; for what are hearts or the words of men before awakening to divine life? And yet grace follows the path of human things. Our faith is awakened through contact with the faith of those from whom we have received our life, our early instruction, and our education. The faith as it has been lived by our family or by our friends, its intensity and its special features continue to live on in us.

There is no such thing as an isolated, autonomous faith. We need only imagine for a moment what would happen if all faith should suddenly cease to exist around us. I do not mean that the world should suddenly become hostile to our faith; for hostility in itself implies a relationship; it can kindle, it can arouse even to the point of risking all. That is not what I mean. Let us imagine a climate of indifference, or rather of complete indifference. Could we really be believers in such an atmosphere? Would we keep our faith? Nothing is impossible to God, but experience teaches us that in such an atmosphere faith would never be born—and even if it were, it would be frozen to death, like a tiny plant on a glacier.

Our personal faith draws its life from the totality of faith around us, which goes back from the present into the past; but that means the Church.

"The Church" means the "us" in faith; it is the sum total, the whole community of believers; it is the believing collectivity. It is not merely Christian prayer which ought to say "us," but also faith. The latter is equally rooted in "us," understood as a whole. The true "us" is more than a mere sum of individuals. It is a movement proceeding from them all. A true collectivity or totality is something more than a simple grouping of a few individuals; it is a vast living structure of which each individual is a member. A hundred men who stand before God as an *ekklesia* represent something more than the mere addition of a hundred individuals; they constitute a living and believing community—we do not mean merely a simple "community" in the purely subjective sense of the term, a convenient designation for a feeling arising from the communal needs of the individual. No, the origin of the community we are referring to here, its consistency and its value, are drawn from something outside the communal needs of the individual; they come from elsewhere, they derive consistency and value from elsewhere: I refer to the "Church."[1]

The Church is the institution planted by Christ in history, amidst mankind. It embraces not "several individuals" or even "all individuals"—these are mere numerical aggregates—but the whole human race as such, humanity in its entirety. The latter has been called to a holy life and to a new birth on the day of Pentecost. This Christian totality is something concrete and real and would continue to exist, even were it, from the point of

1.   Cf. Guardini, *The Meaning of the Church* (Providence: Cluny, 2018).

view of numbers, reduced to but three members. It is not the result of the will or thought of men—the existence of the Christian individual is not either—but it exists by virtue of a divine decree, by a holy institution and creation according to the will of Christ.

The Church founded by Christ, the bearer of His word, speaks to the individual with authority. "If he refuse to hear even the Church, let him be to you as the heathen and the publican." It is for each individual the sphere of his Christian life. In it "we are no longer strangers, but dwellers in the same house." It is the choir in which individuals each have their place; it is a believing totality, militant, offering, celebrating. It is the unity of the holy life in which each shares; it is the body after having been the womb which bore him.

In it the redeeming power of God has got hold of the roots of existence. The new creation has begun to exist in it. New heavens and a new earth; we might almost say a "new nature," only now true nature, made possible by grace.

The Church is the spouse of Christ and the holy mother of each believer. At the announcement of the Word and at the baptismal font its entrails are opened: a new birth comes into being, deriving from God. It is to it, and not to the life of the individual, that the "efficacious signs" belong, the sacraments; it is to it that the forms and sacred rules of the new life belong, in which the individual "penetrates."

The Church itself believes. It lives by believing. The faith of the Church has a character all its own. It is all-embracing, manifold, yet remains one; full of tensions, formed of afterthoughts, and yet constitutes a whole. The faith of the Church is rooted and realized in other structures of mind and soul than the faith of the individual. It has a profundity and a greatness which are peculiar to it; it is exposed to crises which are peculiar to it. (This is not the place to go into these matters.)

It is in this life of faith of the Church that the individual shares, and in different ways.

The Church is the original principle from which the life of the individual comes; it is the ground which supports him, the atmosphere which he breathes—and we thus return to the answer we heard at the beginning of our study and could not yet understand: the Church is a living whole which penetrates the individual. It is from it that he draws his life, without needing to know why. But the "Church" can also be aloof from the individual, pull itself together, and face him, the repository of a sacred authority. This is what it does when it teaches, distinguishes, judges or commands.

It is to the Church, not to the individual, that the new life is entrusted—the divine teaching, the mystery of Christ, and the sacred government; and there is likewise conferred on it the creative power to transmit and to propagate the faith.

The role of the Church is entirely material: it bears us, it is the ground which supports us, and the atmosphere in which we live. Of course, it is God who is working through it; but through the intermediary of the Church He gives to the individual the content of faith and the power to believe. By recapitulating all, it becomes a teacher, and by exercising authority, it becomes a judge. Here also it is God who acts through it, through it alone and not through individuals, even though they be the most gifted and intelligent of persons. It is through the intermediary of the Church that God teaches and judges the faith of the individual, according to the word: "He who refuses to hear even the Church, let him be to you as the heathen and the publican."

This double meaning of Church—to live in each believer as the latter lives in it—to be imposed on him by its teaching and its laws—appears in the case of dogma with a particular sharpness.

The Church believes, and it is substantially the same with it as with the person who lives without being conscious of the fact. But once he encounters an obstacle or a danger, he then becomes aware of what he is doing and changes his attitude; he reflects and becomes responsible. It is the same in the case of the Church: the Church believes without being especially aware of the rich content of its faith. It lives in the world of faith, simply, as people live in the world of things. It lives on in the history of its faith, simply, as people do in the course of their natural lives. But suddenly a question arises in connection with a trend of the age, or a crisis develops with reference to the religious beliefs of certain individuals or groups: for example, the relationship between grace and the natural capacity of man, or the essential nature of the mystery of the Eucharist, etc. Then it does what every endangered life does: it recoils, it withdraws from the crowd. It becomes aware of what is at stake, and distinguishes the true meaning of the conviction of faith from the false meaning. In order to do this it may elaborate its teaching with more precision or fix it in a solemn definition, such as the symbols of faith (*Credo*) which were recited by all before the reception of the neophytes in baptism. It may also distinguish truth from error with regard to a particular point, with an incisive logic, and then we have a *dogma* properly speaking, the *lex credendi*, the rule of faith.

"Dogma" means that the faith of the Church has become acutely aware of itself, that it has separated itself from a false concept and also given itself a precise meaning. Dogma is thus nothing else than the believing Church itself, at the moment when it protects its life of faith with extreme clearness and forcefulness, by imposing on the individual the "rule of faith."

The aim of dogma is always the same: to preserve in its entirety the mystery of Revelation. That which comes from God the holy—the incomprehensible, Master of all truth, independent of the world—cannot be grasped by mere human reason. This mystery is not merely beyond him, it lifts man out of his self-complacency and places him in the wrong. Here we have the critical point about Revelation; it is that against which man revolts. Every dogmatic error is basically directed against mystery. It always tries, in one way or another, from one viewpoint or another, to dissolve the mystery of Revelation. That is not always immediately apparent. Heresies are always propagated by very religious men. They are men who mean well. They see more deeply; bring to light what has become obscured; struggle against an impoverishment of the Christian life or some abuse; they are serious and enthusiastic individuals. Hence we often feel a sympathy for them—just as we are inclined to dislike the authority which opposes them, all the more so in that its representatives are more often than not unworthy people and during the struggle the worst human characteristics seem to come to the fore—it is not for nothing that the word "orthodoxy" has acquired such a distasteful meaning. Yet this does not prevent what we have said above from being true, that the final aim of heresy, even that which is propagated with the best of intentions and which seems bound up with the noblest of human qualities, is to destroy the holy mystery of Revelation and thus annihilate faith.

Revelation means that the word of God penetrates the human sphere and must therefore transcend the mind of man. But this transcendence is the foundation of his salvation and it is important that the mystery be preserved. Heresies always arise from particular circumstances: from certain ideas, attitudes, patterns, tendencies of the day—and in spite of profound thought, penetrating criticism and noble impulses. Ultimately, when ideas and actions have had their say, we find that the mysterious structure of the truth of faith has been disrupted.

It is this which dogma opposes. We often hear it said: Dogmas are mere rationalizations, pure conceptualizations of that which ought to remain living. He who says this shows that he has not understood what they are about. Of course, dogmas contain ideas and abstract thoughts; but if we look more closely to see how these thoughts are put together and how the different ideas are related to one another, we see that they are placed around the mystery in order to protect it. The dogma is a solid fortress or protective ring surrounding the source, the depth, the life.

Dogma confronts the individual. It is here that the opposition of the Church, mentioned above, can reveal itself in a particularly harsh light as regards the individual. Either one of two things may happen: either the believer recognizes that it is really the Church which is speaking and Christ through it, and that he who hears the Church hears Christ; realizing and admitting that each believer "must lose himself in order to find himself"— or he rejects everything. Then the faith of the individual breaks with the community; not only with the community of a small circle, or a group, or a movement, but with the living totality of the Church. Then his faith truly becomes individual in the worst sense of the term—a peculiar faith, a "heresy" (Greek *hairesis*, "choice").

But if one who is confronted by a decision of this kind recognizes that it is a question of a trial; if he accepts what is offered to him; if he is capable of making, in all sincerity, the often very difficult sacrifice of his own personal opinion in the face of dogma, persuaded that it is Christ Himself who is speaking in the dogma through His Church—then the dogma penetrates him. That which at first collided with him from outside—with all that rocklike hardness which is peculiar to the Church when it combats, mixed up with human mediocrity, narrow-mindedness, despotism, violence, the obstinacy of individuals who are determined to be right and to triumph, and all the rest which is likely to occur in such cases—the dogma becomes an integral part of his life. It becomes for him space, order, strength. From then on it is the dogma which determines his life in all its aspects. The dogma supports and enlightens him; like the ground beneath his feet on which the believer stands; like a living form within him, which guides his steps in the world.

This clash with dogma may have its very humiliating side. The judgment and feelings of the individual may be violently opposed to the "rule of faith" and the human manner in which it is proposed—but there can scarcely be any experience so reassuring and comforting as that in which the believer leans on dogma, and relying upon it, confronts the world.

Faith, as a faculty of immediate intuition or aggressive and creative capacity, is often found opposed to dogma, which is accused of chilling and killing the Christian life. This can happen of course, has happened in fact, and living faith has died; or perhaps it has no longer succeeded in attaching itself to the dogmatic element and has proceeded on its own way. That is why all those who speak for dogma have such a great responsibility. But the sharp division and decision of dogma must exist nevertheless. The historical existence of the Church, which passes incessantly from spontaneousness to awareness and the responsibility which flows from this, demands that. And the life of the individual also demands it; for however fine a thing spontaneity of life may be—the time will necessarily come when we must stand firm, choose, take sides. Faith also involves maturity, character, and coming of age. Properly understood and lived, dogma really means character in faith. Upon encountering dogma, a spontaneous and living faith may also become involved in a crisis. We must resign ourselves to this as something inevitable. But if faith always emerges victorious, if it assimilates dogma, it then acquires a spirit of decision and an awareness of responsibility and of destiny which are simply irreplaceable. It need not lose its vibrant energy. It has only to gain by the seriousness and pain of discussion.

This is the way faith broadens and matures, until finally dogma gradually penetrates the life and attitude of the believer. It penetrates to the extent that—except at certain moments of warning and demand—it influences the life of the believer, no longer mainly as a conscious directive force or rule, but more as a guide on the road toward a higher liberty.

X

Faith and the Church: Sacrament

WE have asked ourselves what the Church means to the believer. We have seen that the faith of individuals is bound up with that of others; that its content always comes to it from other believers; and that because of this there is a continual tension which is peculiar to it. Faith does not derive its origin from what is human, of course; God is the one who awakens faith—but He awakens it in the human being, and man is thus for man the road which leads to God.

We have also seen that the faith of the individual is formed in the faith of the community; there is the same faith for the Church itself and for the individual belonging to it. The individual believes and it is by him that the Church believes. The Church not only stands before him, but is in him; it is present in the roots of that divine life which comes to him from God, there, namely, where the "I" and the "we," the individual and society, form but one living whole.

Finally, we have seen how the Church comes to define dogmas, in self-defense and conflict; we have seen how these confront the individual, and how once accepted, they become the basis of his personal faith.

We must now look at the question from another point of view.

In the Epistles of St. Paul the Apostle faith is often closely linked with baptism, to such an extent that the two things seem to be identified. It seems that "to be baptized" and "to believe" mean the same thing. Or, baptism may be represented as the planting of a seed, the immediate effect of which is faith. What does baptism mean? It is not merely the incorporation of the individual in the community, nor the consecration of his act of adherence, nor the act whereby the community assumes responsibility for the neophyte. Something much more profound occurs in baptism: a seed of life is formed. In the man who had hitherto lived from a purely worldly point of view, God implants the seed of a new structure and a new activity. A new life is awakened in him, with its own meaning, its own law, and its own power of realization. A wild fruit tree draws strength from its natural environment; as soon as the gardener grafts something onto it, that is, introduces a new element from some other living thing into it, the old tree is able to bear new fruit. The fruit belongs to the old tree, but only because it has received a new vitality from some other living thing. This may serve to illustrate what happens in baptism; except that the penetration is here much more complete and profound. The root of life itself, the very center of our existence, is seized and drawn into the divine bosom in order to receive from there a new vitality. That is done through Christ. Man is reborn in Him, by the Holy Spirit, in order to share in the human and divine life of Christ. From then on man builds his own life, acts, believes and loves, and it is of course he himself who is doing the living; his whole human nature is manifested and expressed by his works—but what counts above all in the sight of God and eternity is something else, the essential thing in fact: the new source, the life of Christ, Christ risen in him. It is only when man has given himself wholly to Christ who calls him, that he becomes in truth himself, such as God wishes him to be.

But how are we to describe this state of the regenerated man? Certainly not as an isolated individual, but rather as the member of a whole, of the Church. On the purely natural level men are of course not mere individuals, unattached specimens: they always stand in relationship to each other. Each one is not only attracted by the others, forms connections, alienates his own autonomy, but there is manifested in all individuals a totality which embraces them all. Human nature involves participation in a collective life, namely, the human race, which is divided into races, nations, and families. It is under this social aspect of existence that humanity as such participates in the new birth. That is what happened at Pentecost when the Holy Spirit intervened in the course of world history, inaugurating the Christian era. This is what happens each time that the word of the Gospel is directed to a nation as a "whole," and during all the various acts of worship in which a parish participates. And this is what happens continually in the rebirth of the individual, for this "whole" is in him, we may even say that he is this "whole," to the extent that his life is directed toward it. But the social life which issues from this rebirth is, with respect to the individual, the other element of the Christian life: the Church. This of course gathers all the individuals together, but it remains in spite of everything independent of numbers, since "two or three gathered in the name of Christ" suffice to constitute it. In the Church we find the same new image: Christ; the same new force: grace; the same spiritual power: the Holy Spirit. And in spite of the human, one may even say too human, character of the Church, we may say that it is the divine life which is acting in the life of the Church, in its manifestations of itself and in its history.[1]

The Christian self founded on baptism moves by faith toward him from whom it has derived its origin. But it does not do so as an individual, cut off from others; it carries the others along with it, it carries everybody along, even if it is not actually aware of this explicitly.

The individual bears the Church in his faith, both its dynamic power and its weight; the Church is present to him as it is. It bears him and weighs him down. Its life nourishes him. Its immensity humbles him. Its breadth enlarges his horizon; its wisdom gives him a rule of life; its power enlarges his field of activity. Its formalism blocks him; its coldness hardens him; and whatever is violent, selfish, hard or vulgar about the Church has an influence upon the faith of the individual, so that the latter sometimes seems obliged to sustain the cause of God, not only in the darkness of the world, but also in that of the Church. Of course we have the free surging of the soul in mystery face to face with God alone. But even this colloquy does not take place in a void. Where it has its roots, there also are to be found the roots of the Church.

1.   Cf. also, Guardini, *Meaning of the Church*.

To wish to ignore all these inherent weaknesses would not be a mark of love or loyalty. It would to reveal one's own superficiality. The most loving and loyal believers have always been those who understood profoundly the painful identity of these two sides of the Church.

St. Paul connects faith intimately with baptism. We find a similar linking of two things in St. John, namely, faith and the Eucharist.

In the sixth chapter of his Gospel which describes the promise at Capernaum, the Lord speaks of the "true bread" which the Father gives and which He Himself is. It will be given by preaching and received by hearing. To believe is to eat spiritually, to receive the divine life offered in the Word. That is what the Lord is speaking about at first; then the meaning of His words changes, and "bread" is not merely the spiritual content of the message, but the holy meal of the Eucharist. And "eating" is no longer the fact of believing, but the fulfillment of the sacrament in faith.

St. John combines faith and eucharistic nourishment in the same way St. Paul does faith and baptism. To believe and to eat are, so to speak, different forms, different states of the same basic act: the living communication of man turned toward God with the essential Truth, such as the Father offers it in Christ.

The form of the repast already suggests that it is no longer merely a question of an individual. According to its original meaning the word "meal" denotes a collective event. Those who gather together eat their meal and in so doing become one; for the meal has the mysterious power of binding the guests together. This was the idea of a meal in times past when people were still conscious of the fundamental meaning underlying simple human acts. It was a premonition, a portion of the original prophecy inscribed on creation, on the realities and symbols of existence, pointing to Christ, the Logos. Here, at the table of the Lord, the prophecy is fulfilled. All eat the same holy nourishment, all are united together in it, as that beautiful passage from the "Teaching of the Twelve Apostles" (*Didache*) puts it, where it is said that many grains have had to be gathered together to form the unity of bread, just as the juice of many grapes must flow together in order to form the one stream which is wine.

For the same Christ who nourishes each one is also the life of the Church. He lives in all these men not only as the form and inner reality of the individual, but also as the constructive image and pulsating force of the whole. It is through Him that humanity, considered as a whole, becomes Christian, the living totality of God which is the Church, the "body of Christ." However, as soon as man eats the holy supper the "Church" begins to live in him; in himself, in his neighbor, in someone else and so on in others, "that all may be one" in Christ.

More than this, St. Augustine gives expression to the beautiful thought that it is not the communicant who takes Christ to himself, but actually Christ who "eats" and "incorporates" the communicant. Christ living in the Church is continuously receiving the individual into the communion of His life, whenever the mystery of the Eucharist is celebrated.

Faith is a communication of man with God in Christ. But it is not the isolated individual who communicates here with Christ, but the totality of which the individual forms but a part; and in the same Christ, all the individuals taken together who constitute this totality.

Moreover, the relationship is reversed, and it becomes the vast totality of the Church which seizes the individual and carries him along on the road toward God.

Here we have the communal element of faith revealed in another light, namely in the sacramental, the Mystery (*sacramentum = mysterion,* "mystery").

Believing is not merely action, thought, willing, behavior; it involves the essence of being. More precisely, belief means that the created being is on the road toward God. It is this process which, coming from God, takes hold of the being of man, namely the new birth, the invasion of divine love or of divine life from which a new existence comes to be by the grace of God—and the newborn man then makes this process personally his own in the tension of faith. Faith is a movement which is continually being born in the mystery of that transubstantiation which takes place in the sacrament.

But in this mystery it is not a question of individual existence. God takes hold of humanity and the individual in it. He grasps the individual, but only in the whole. He grasps the whole, that is the Church, in order to get at the individual through it; or again, the individual in order that the Church may be.

God visits man redeemed by Christ and brings him back to Himself. It is He Himself, we are even tempted to say, who believes in place of man. In the process of regeneration He gives man His own life that it may become man's life; in faith, the one who has become a Christian returns to God, but it is the life of God which draws him.

But is faith not one of the "theological virtues"? Let us not forget the forceful primary meaning of the word: a virtue of God. That holy efficaciousness, that is, that eminent activity of which God alone is capable and which consists in understanding Himself as holy, personal truth; this is the virtue which He also exercises in and through men. In doing so, He gives it to them, "pours it into them," as it were. And then it is they who indeed believe, but God who "believes" in them.

Let us be more down to earth. Let us abandon these high-flown expressions and say simply: God creates the mystery of the communion with Himself which we call faith on earth. Some day, in the light of eternity, this mystery will be called vision.

Yet faith and vision are both mere words or symbols by which we attempt to express the inexpressible. God grant that we may be able to share in this mystery both now and forever and ever. Amen.

CLUNY MEDIA

Designed by Fiona Cecile Clarke, the CLUNY MEDIA *logo*
depicts a monk at work in the scriptorium,
with a cat sitting at his feet.

The monk represents our mission to emulate
the invaluable contributions of the monks
of Cluny in preserving the libraries of the West,
our strivings to know and love the truth.

The cat at the monk's feet is Pangur Bán, from the
eponymous Irish poem of the 9th century.
The anonymous poet compares his scholarly
pursuit of truth with the cat's happy hunting of mice.
The depiction of Pangur Bán is an homage to the work
of the monks of Irish monasteries and a sign
of the joy we at Cluny take in our trade.

"Messe ocus Pangur Bán,
cechtar nathar fria saindan:
bíth a menmasam fri seilgg,
mu memna céin im saincheirdd."

Made in the USA
Monee, IL
30 October 2023

45447494R00083